Merchandising Mathematics
Revised First Edition

Merchandising Mathematics
Revised First Edition

ANTIGONE KOTSIOPULOS, Ph.D.

Professor Emeritus
Colorado State University

JOAN ANDERSON, Ph.D.

Associate Professor
Washington State University

JIKYEONG KANG, Ph.D.

Manchester Business School

FAIRCHILD BOOKS, INC.

New York

Director of Sales and Acquisitions: Dana Meltzer-Berkowitz

Executive Editor: Olga T. Kontzias

Senior Development Editor: Jennifer Crane

Art Director: Adam B. Bohannon

Production Manager: Ginger Hillman

Associate Production Editor: Jessica Rozler

Software Developer: Cindy Zayas

Cover Design: Adam B. Bohannon

Text Design and Page Composition: GEX Publishing Services

Library of Congress Catalog Card Number: 2007943508
ISBN: 978-1-56367-675-8
GST R 133004424
Printed in the United States of America
TP09

Brief Contents

Extended Contents

Preface

Merchandising Mathematics began as a software program generating "story problems" for students. It replaced hours of problem development and grading deemed necessary for the mastery of basic principles and terminology. Eventually, written documentation was added and ultimately the text and software were published. **This revised first edition of** Merchandising Mathematics **provides a major upgrade to the programming utilized for generating problems, providing help messages, and evaluating student performance.** All of this was done with the belief that sound basic math and communication skills are vital to the success of those involved in merchandising and retailing arenas.

My professional life has permitted me to work for small specialty stores, as well as large department and specialty operations. I also worked on a product development team with programmers and engineers to develop a turnkey system for small retailers. As a faculty member, I have developed curriculum, coordinated internships, provided workshops and seminars for business and industry, and currently serve as a department head. I have seen a great deal of change in merchandising practices and procedures over time and among different product areas and business sectors. It is impossible to represent all perspectives, but we believe that we have selected what are the most common, current practices.

When you are first examining this text and software, please refer to the introduction (*How to Use the Text and Software*) on page xvi. The introduction will take you through some of the basic math skills that you need to know to successfully use this text as well as giving you step-by-step instructions on how the software program works. To learn how to install the software, please refer to the software installation instructions on page xxi. As you work through the text and use the software, we encourage you to show how you work the problems. Be less concerned about having the exact answer and more concerned about understanding the concepts. Rounding and math errors can occur at any point. The computer does not round during the process, but rather, it rounds at the end of the process. If you can show how you solved the problem, you can demonstrate your understanding of the computation no matter whether your answer is technically "correct" or not.

This book is presented in six chapters, starting with basic markups and markdowns and ending with profit and loss statements. In *Chapter One—Making a Profit*, the various methods of calculating markup are discussed including individual, cumulative, average, initial, and maintained markup. You are shown how to figure dollars and percentage markups. Although most markup is calculated at retail, the cost method also is explained.

In *Chapter Two—Reducing the Retail Price*, you are instructed on how and why retail prices are reduced. Markdowns are the most frequent means of reducing the retail price and the text covers broad areas of the reasons for this type of price adjustment. Employee and customer discounts also reduce the retail price. Because some unsold items may be returned to their original price or an alternate price, you will learn how to calculate the net effect of a markdown, as well as markdown cancellations.

Locating suitable merchandise for the customer is only part of a buyer's responsibilities. An equally important responsibility—and one that certainly will impact business profitability—is negotiating with the vendor. The vendor represents the manufacturer in the distribution process. In *Chapter Three—Discounts, Terms, and Datings*, the quantitative aspects of negotiating are explored. As a buyer places an order, the cooperative advertising money, the logistics (i.e., how and when) the merchandise will be packaged and shipped, and what special pricing or shipping agreements can be negotiated.

When retailers refer to inventory or stock, they are referring to the merchandise they have in their store. A key to successful business planning is to have the appropriate merchandise at the right time, in the right place, and in the right quantities to meet consumer needs and wants. This may sound like a simple request, but the planning and attainment of this goal is complicated and often difficult to achieve. *Chapter Four—Assessing Stock Activity*, will expose you to the basic elements involved in monitoring the success of stock planning. Determining the amount of merchandise available at any point in time, calculating inventory, and ascertaining stock shortages are examined in detail. Additionally, calculating such financial ratios as stock turnover and stock-sales ratios, which are used to compare the performance of one business or department with another, are covered fully.

Some of the mathematical tools mentioned will be used to develop a merchandising plan or budget, which is presented in *Chapter Five—Planning Merchandising Budgets*. Such a budget is most commonly planned for a six-month period, but also can be broken down by months or weeks. While formats and specific elements of merchandising plans may vary, the principal components are used by all retailers for planning and decision making.

Up to this point in the book, each chapter evolves around a specific concept or procedure. In *Chapter Six—Maximizing Profit*, all these concepts are merged to provide a working example of how various mathematical tools contribute to the total business performance picture. A profit and loss statement serves as a summary of the business activities for a particular period and, of course, reflects business profit or loss.

As you work through sections of the book answering the sample problems and using the software drills for practice, always keep in mind that each of the mathematical tools explored reflects its purpose or impacts on profit. This realization is vital to merchandising success. We have made the assumption that you, the user of this book, have minimal to no knowledge of these tools, but if there has been some exposure, it will serve to accelerate your learning pace.

ACKNOWLEDGMENTS

Joan L. Anderson, Ph.D., and Cindy Zayas are key parties in the creation of the revised first edition of this text. This text is unique, because of its software component, which has been totally rewritten for this edition. Based on our direction, Cindy Zayas wrote the new software. Joan Anderson and her students completed major testing of the new software. I am indebted to both.

Joan Anderson completed her baccalaureate and masters degrees at Colorado State University in Design and Merchandising, and received her Ph.D. from CSU in the School of Education. A component of her work at CSU involved testing software and writing documentation. She obtained experience in the technology industry by teaching and training retailers who purchased turnkey computer systems. Joan is currently an Associate Professor of Apparel, Merchandising, Design and Textiles, at Washington State University. Cindy Zayas completed her baccalaureate degree at Colorado State University in the area of computer science. She is currently employed as a senior program analyst in Colorado Springs, Colorado.

There are many people to thank for making this publication possible and it is impossible to name everyone. I am personally grateful to all of my senior and graduate students over the years who helped me grade problems manually and who helped me to the realization that this book and software had to be published. Consequently, I thank past students like Sam Kaufman, now owner of Kaufman's Tall and Big, one of the most successful specialty operations of its type in the country. Additionally, graduate students like Joan Lascoe, Chris Biere, Joan Anderson, and Sarita Kurvilla helped us enormously by working out bugs and solution sets. The internship program at Colorado State University has provided excellent opportunities for our students and faculty to learn about industry practices and procedures. We thank all the manufacturers, wholesalers, and retailers who have worked with our students and who have provided us with valuable training information and perspectives.

It is impossible for us to find out all the institutions that purchased earlier versions of *Merchandising Mathematics*, but the hundreds of purchases through Kinko's made us believe there was a big enough demand to pursue publication. Special thanks to the students who used the text and software (in its different incarnations) from the University of Nebraska, University of Minnesota, and of course, Colorado State University. Several faculty members took the time to provide extensive feedback and to test the product in different computer lab environments. For their comments, recommendations, and encouragement, we would like to thank Wanda Cheek, Molly Eckman, Judy Everett, Bettie Minshall, and Elizabeth Csordas. Thank you for your diligence and input which allowed us to make valuable changes and corrections. To the reviewers provided by the publisher—Grace I. Kunz, Laura Jolly, Deborah Fowler, and Cindi Baker—thank you for your diligence and the thoroughness of your input, which allowed us to make valuable changes and corrections.

A great deal of credit and appreciation is extended to Jikyeong Kang, Ph.D., who was a graduate student at CSU during my early years teaching there and persuaded me to seek a publisher for the book. She engaged me in the venture by agreeing to convert the programs from the mainframe into appropriate language for the first microcomputers used at Colorado State and thus became my first co-author. Jikyeong Kang, Ph.D. received her masters degree with a specialization in merchandising and attained her doctorate at the University of Minnesota. Dr. Kang is currently a professor and Director of Graduate Programs at the Manchester Business School London, in the United Kingdom.

Special thanks to Jean Raney for creation of the instructor's guide and Judy Rogers and Jess Kampen for manuscript preparation. I would also like to thank Susan Jeffers Casel, our first editor at Fairchild Books, for her attention to details, clarity in communication, notes of encouragement, and her ability to be so specific with schedule and timelines. Fairchild Books should also be recognized for its willingness to be among the first to experiment with the publication of software. Without help from all of these entities, there may not have been a first edition.

Last but not least, I want to acknowledge the University of Nebraska-Lincoln, and specifically Ann Parkhurst, who taught me the power of computing in the early 1970s. Without the availability of free and easy access to computer technology and consulting, thousands of students would have been denied this creative and effective method for learning merchandising mathematics.

ANTIGONE KOTSIOPULOS, PH.D.
Professor Emeritus
Colorado State University
2008

Objectives for Merchandising Mathematics

CALCULATE AND DEFINE

- The five types of markup: individual, initial, average, cumulative, and maintained.
- Retail price reductions in dollars and percentages.
- Net sales, cost of goods sold, gross margin, operating expenses, and profit.
- Invoice prices given terms of sale and dating terms.
- Trade, quantity, and cash discounts.
- Turnover and stock-sales ratio.
- Planned purchases at retail and cost.
- Open-to-buy in dollars and units.
- Planned sales, stocks, markups, and markdowns for completion of a six-month plan.

UNDERSTAND AND IDENTIFY

- The relationship of the three elements in pricing goods to make a profit: retail, cost, and markup.
- The equations used to determine retail, cost, and markup dollars and percentages.
- Discounts and markdowns, which are used to reduce the retail price.
- The effect on markup and profit when the retail price is reduced.
- Various dating terms on an invoice.
- Book inventory and physical inventory.
- The format and the basic elements of a profit and loss statement and how they are related in determining a final profit or loss figure.

DISCUSS AND EXPLAIN

- Various reasons for retail reductions, stock shortages, and overages.
- External and internal factors that affect planned sales.
- Turnover and the causes for being high or low.
- The elements in planning a merchandise budget and its importance to business operations.
- Three primary ways to increase operating profit.

How to Use the Text and Software

Mathematical skills are essential to anyone interested in competing in career areas that deal with product development, distribution, merchandising, or retailing. The purpose of this book is to introduce mathematical tools that will aid in merchandise selection and selling by using quantitative and qualitative criteria. Those in positions of merchandising responsibility and authority are constantly asking:

- What merchandise should be kept on hand to meet the needs and wants of the consumer?

- At what price or price levels should the merchandise be sold to the consumer?

- What quantities, colors, and sizes should be made available to the consumer?

- When should the product be introduced to the public?

Some of these questions may be answered by guesswork, but a more profitable method is to replace guesswork with homework. Some people believe that the retailing function of satisfying the needs and wants of the consumer is accomplished with luck, a feel for the business, or good taste. These three attributes are indeed a part of the success of a retailing business, but are certainly not the key elements.

The function of this book is not to teach you how to be a buyer or how to run a retail operation. The purpose of this text is to provide an overview of basic math functions that are used by buyers and store owners to operate their businesses, stores, or departments profitably. Not all the formulas will be used by all store owners, retailers, and buyers, and because of the nature of retailing and the diversity of the different businesses that sell goods, there are even different names that are given to the same activity or formula. However, if you understand the concept you will be able to transfer your knowledge and understanding to any new situation.

The initial assumption made by the authors is that you have minimal knowledge of basic mathematical tools. Each subdivision of a chapter emphasizes the use of a different mathematical tool. Tools, like game rules, must be adapted to memory and be understood clearly to be completely effective. The better you know the rules and the tools, the more instinctive your reactions become, and the quicker you will be able to respond to the many stressful situations that are a part of the buyer's or retailer's life. If the "game" you are playing is merchandising, the object of the game is to create profit. Regardless of how much you want to win a game or to increase profit, you can not do it effectively or consistently unless you have the proper tools. If you have been exposed to some of them, this merely accelerates your learning pace. A clear understanding of each new formula is advisable before proceeding to a more challenging one. It is also important for you to recognize how the tools might be utilized in an applied setting. If you read and completely understand the components of this book you will have the essential mathematical foundations for effective planning and monitoring of your business.

Information concerning the application of mathematics in a retail setting has been disseminated in a variety of publications with various levels of sophistication. A number of factors make our publication unique. All problem solving in this text begins on an elementary level and increases in difficulty. This allows flexibility in lesson planning, which depends on the learning level of each group. In some situations, a self-paced approach is implemented, which allows students to work at their own rate. The text provides motivation for the use of each concept and the derivation of each formula is explained carefully. Primary formulas are highlighted and example problems are worked out in detail to demonstrate the use of the formula. In many cases, the solutions illustrate how various concepts interrelate with one another.

All of the major mathematical formulas presented in this book will be brought together and utilized in a the merchandising plan or budget, which is presented in Chapter Five. This budget is planned most commonly for a six-month period, but also can be broken down into individual months or weeks. The six-month merchandise plan is used by most retailers and is explained in full in Chapter Five. As you move through the text, you may want to refer to the merchandising plan on page 140 to find where certain concepts or information would fit into the form.

SOFTWARE AND ASSIGNMENTS REVIEW

At the end of each section, a set of assignments is provided so the student can practice using the concepts presented in that section. Additionally, a package of computer programs is provided for drill and practice on all concepts presented. These programs are unique because all have a number of randomly selected variables. For example, in any given computer problem, the product, price, and quantity will change, but the structure of the problem itself will remain the same. This changeability provides variety for the student and increases the availability of problem generation for the instructor.

The **MerchMath 2.0 Software** will run on any IBM or compatible computer. To access the software after installation, from the desktop, select Start > All Programs > Merchandising. You may have a short cut icon on your desktop. It depends on the way that the program was installed on your computer. After accessing or double clicking on the program, you will be directed to a login screen. Enter your name in the first box, tab or click to the next box and enter your student ID. You MUST enter both your name and student ID before you can proceed. The login screen also has spaces for "class" and "other". These fields are optional. You can proceed to the next screen by pressing enter or clicking on "next".

You are taken to a screen where 25 drills are available. To access a drill, select the drop-down menu for the corresponding chapter. Select the drill you want by highlighting it. You have three options. By selecting "Problems", the system will automatically generate problems for you to practice. The "Exam" session will allow you to enter the number of exam problems you want. You can also select "final" as another testing option. When selecting final, do not preselect a drill—the final is a collection of all problems in the section. In the exam function, a status report will be displayed directly below the problem, showing the number of correct solutions and the total number of problems that you attempted to solve. You can elect to exit the drill or exam at any time.

The computer software that accompanies this book will provide you with a variety of problems related to each chapter and section. The store names, products, and figures are all generated randomly by the software. Therefore you will not be able to check homework with someone else in the class. Additionally, a printout of your performance report that tells how many problems were worked and the percentage of correct answers are also available. The software also has a "help" option that will produce the basic formula for answering the problem. In other words, the computer will give the basic formula, but you may have to rewrite the formula to solve for the unknown. The following examples may serve as a demonstration and reminder of how to solve for the unknown.

The formula: $a = b/c$ could represent $10 = 40/4$; to solve for b, if you know a and c, rewrite it as: $b = a \times c$ or $40 = 10 \times 4$; to solve for c, if you know a and b, rewrote ot as: $c = b/a$ or $4 = 40/10$.

This concept also is applied throughout the book. Each chapter introduces basic formulas. From the basic formulas, other equations are derived as the student solves for the unknown quantities.

MATH REVIEW

Most problems in this book require the understanding and use of fractions, decimals, or percentages. These three terms are used to express parts of a whole, such as sales, inventory, and retail price. The basic mathematical concepts that are essential to understanding this book are reviewed here, as follows:

1. A fraction is part of a whole and is used to state the relation of one or more parts to the number of the whole. A fraction is written as:

   $\dfrac{1 \text{ (numerator)}}{10 \text{ (denominator)}}$ — number of parts under consideration.

   — number of parts into which the item is divided.

2. A decimal is a fraction in which the denominator is 10, 100, 1000, or some multiple of 10. Instead of writing the denominator, it is indicated by the decimal point and the number of digits to the right, as in:

   $$\frac{1}{10} = .1 \qquad \frac{1}{100} = 0.1 \qquad \frac{1}{1000} = .001$$

3. Any fraction can be written as a decimal even though the denominator is not a multiple of 10, and is found by dividing the numerator by the denominator, as in:

   $$5\overline{)1.00}^{\,.20} \text{ or } \frac{1}{5} = .20$$

4. Percentages are another way of expressing parts of a whole. A percentage is a decimal where the denominator is 100, and the whole is 100/100, therefore, $25/100 = .25$. To express a decimal as a percent, multiply the decimal by 100% (or move the decimal point two places to the right and add the percent sign).

5. Parenthesis are used in mathematical formulas to guide the sequence of computations. Those computations in parenthesis should be performed first.

6. When and how you round a number can make a difference in the mathematical outcome. The software program will not round off numbers during sequential operations. It will round only the final number, to the designated number of digits. In the text, our rule is to round four places after the decimal in the illustrated problems. Final answers are rounded to two decimal places. When working computer generated problems, use your calculator and avoid rounding until you have the final answer. In this manner, your answer should match, or be closer to the computer's computation. The software also has a feature on more complete solutions that will accept answers within a small percentage of error. This feature should minimize errors due to rounding.

MerchMath 2.0 Software Installation Instructions

System Requirements

The MerchMath 2.0 software will run on any IBM or compatible computer that is running Windows 98 Second Edition, Windows NT 4.0, Windows 2000, or Windows XP. The software requires a minimum of 32MB of RAM and 10MB of space available on the hard drive. The best monitor resolution for this program is 800 × 600 pixels or higher.

Setting Modifications

To Change Monitor Resolution: Click on 'Start' located at the bottom left of the screen on the task bar. Then click on 'Settings'. Finally, click on 'Control Panel' and select the 'Display' icon. Once the display window appears, click on the tab named 'Settings', and move the slide rule to 800 × 600 pixels or higher.

Installation

CD-ROM: Insert the MerchMath 2.0 software CD into the CD drive. The system may begin installing the software automatically. In this case, simply follow the instructions on your screen to complete installation. If the system does not begin installing automatically, there are two options for installation.

1. Double click on 'My Computer', which is located on the system's desktop. After the 'My Computer' window is visible, double click on the CD drive. Once the CD drive is open, double click on the computer icon that is labeled 'Setup'. The computer will now automatically install the software.

OR

2. Click the 'Start' button, which is located at the bottom left-hand corner of the screen. Next, click on the option labeled 'Run'. Once the 'Run' dialog box appears, type D:\setup.exe. *Note:* The letter 'D' denotes the CD drive. Once the system starts to install, simply follow the instructions on the screen.

Running the Program:

Once the program is installed, it is ready to use. To begin, click the 'Start' button and select 'Programs'. The MerchMath software is located in the 'Merchandising' folder. Click on the 'Merchandising' folder and then click the MerchMath icon.

Levels

It is recommended that the user start by generating practice problems and exams on the subsection level. Once the subsections are mastered, the user has the option to test and generate problems on the section level. Once the first two levels are mastered, the user can advance to the chapter level, and finally to the final level. To illustrate the level system, a portion of Chapter One is shown:

Chapter level $\rightarrow$ Chapter 1

Section Level $\rightarrow$ Individual Markups

      Subsection Level $\rightarrow$ Basic RCM Relationships

MerchMath 2.0 Instructions

Login Screen

This screen allows the user to input his or her name, ID number, class, and other. While the Name and the ID number fields are required, the class and other fields are optional. The instructor may wish for students to input other information in those fields. For example, it may be required for students to type the teacher's assistant's name in the "Other" field. The login information will be used throughout the course of each session to identify the user. If the user wishes to save any information or print the results of an exam, this information will be supplied on the output.

Main Screen

This screen allows the user to select practice problems, an exam, or a final exam.

Drop Down Lists

There are six drop down lists available. Each list corresponds to a chapter in the *Merchandising Mathematics* textbook. The user has the option to choose any chapter, section, or subsection from any of the drop down lists. However, only one selection can be made.

Problems Button

This option requires the user to choose a chapter, section, or subsection in order to generate practice questions. There is no limit on how many problems the user may choose to have generated. The user may opt to generate 1 question or 10,000 questions.

Exam Button

This option requires the user to choose a chapter, section, or subsection in order to generate exam questions. Once a selection has been made, the user must input the number of questions contained in the exam. The limit of questions on an exam is 50.

Final Button

This option is specifically used to take an exam or generate practice problems over the entire book. The user cannot make any chapter level selections in order to have this option. Once the 'Final' button is selected, the user will have the option to choose either practice problems or an exam. If the 'Practice Problems' option is chosen, an unlimited number of questions can be generated. If an exam is chosen, the user must then input how many questions will be in the exam. The limit of questions on an exam is 50.

Exit Button

This option is used to exit the program.

Notebook Screen

This screen displays program generated exam and practice questions.

Answer Text Box

This text box allows the user to input answers. The input must be numerical and contain only decimal points or negative signs. If the user inputs characters other than a decimal point or a negative sign, the program will consider the answer as incorrect. Examples of unacceptable characters are $, %, *, /.

Submit Button

This option allows the user to submit their answer for verification. Then the program will notify the user if the answer submitted was correct or incorrect.

Solution Button

This option is only available for practice problems. Once selected, a display shows the formula used by the program, the mathematical operations, and the correct answer.

Next Button

This option is only available for practice problems. It allows the user to advance to the next question. The user may choose to stay at a problem for hours, or may choose to skip a problem entirely.

Calculator Button

This option is available on both exams and practice problems. This option opens the system Calculator that is distributed with Windows.

Homework Button

This option allows the user to save homework questions in text format. The user must specify how many questions to be saved. The question limit is 50. The user must specify where the homework will be saved.

Main Menu Button

This option returns the user back to the main menu. Once there, the user may select another option.

Summary Report Screen

This screen allows the user to view the exam summary. The user and exam information is located on the right-hand side of the screen. On the left-hand side of the screen, the user is able to view the entire exam coupled with the correct answers. The user can save the entire exam.

Back and Next Buttons

These options allow the user to navigate through the questions and view any incorrect answers.

Save Button

This option allows the user to save the entire exam. The system saves files in text format.

Main Menu Button

This option allows the user to return to the main menu and make another selection.

Software License Agreement

CD-ROM TERMS AND CONDITIONS OF USE FAIRCHILD BOOKS, INC.

1. License Grant. Fairchild Books, Inc. ("Fairchild"), a division of Condé Nast Publications, hereby grants to you and you accept a limited, non-exclusive license to view and download the data, and use the software on the enclosed CD-ROM *(Merchandising Mathematics)* on a one-at-a-time, serial-use basis, solely for your own personal or internal business use. You agree not to make copies of *Merchandising Mathematics* or to use *Merchandising Mathematics* on an electronic network, including without limitation the Internet and the World Wide Web. If you wish to have concurrent use of *Merchandising Mathematics* you must request a multi-user license from Fairchild. You agree that you will not transfer or sub-license or resell all or any part *of Merchandising Mathematics*. You agree that you will not provide access to *Merchandising Mathematics* or the software or information contained in *Merchandising Mathematics* to any other person or entity, in any way, including but not limited to media, passwords or access codes (other than other users authorized by the institution, where the user is an institution.) You agree that you will not remove or alter the copyright notices or other means of identification or disclaimers as they appear in *Merchandising Mathematics*.

2. Term. This agreement commences on the day you accept the CD-ROM as set forth above. In the event you breach any provision of this agreement, this agreement will automatically terminate in the event you do not cure such breach within three (3) days after such breach.

3. Fairchild Rights. All material contained within this CD-ROM is the sole and exclusive property of Fairchild. By accepting this license you do not become the owner of all or any part *of Merchandising Mathematics*. You agree not to modify or reverse engineer any software received hereunder. To reproduce, republish, upload, post, transmit, adapt, enhance, distribute or publicly display material from this CD-ROM, you will need prior written permission from Fairchild.

4. Disclaimer or Warranty. *Merchandising Mathematics* IS PROVIDED "AS IS" AND WITHOUT WARRANTIES OF ANY KIND, EITHER EXPRESS OR IMPLIED. TO THE FULLEST EXTENT PERMISSIBLE PURSUANT TO APPLICABLE LAW, FAIRCHILD DISCLAIMS ALL WARRANTIES, EXPRESS OR IMPLIED, INCLUDING BUT NOT LIMITED TO IMPLIED WARRANTIES OR MERCHANTABILITY AND FITNESS FOR A PARTICULAR PURPOSE. FAIRCHILD DOES NOT WARRANT OR REPRESENT THAT *Merchandising Mathematics* IS ACCURATE OR RELIABLE OR WILL MEET YOUR REQUIREMENTS OR EXPECTATIONS. FAIRCHILD DOES NOT WARRANT OR REPRESENT THAT

THE CD-ROM WILL OPERATE UNINTERRUPTED OR BE FREE OF ERRORS OR VIRUSES.

5. Limitation of Liability. FAIRCHILD DISCLAIMS ANY AND ALL LIABILITY TO ANY PARTY FOR THE ACCURACY OR CORRECTNESS OF THE INFORMATION IN THE *Merchandising Mathematics* CD-ROM AND WORKBOOK, ANY LOSS OR DAMAGE CAUSED BY FAIRCHILD OR BY ERRORS OR OMISSIONS IN *Merchandising Mathematics* CD-ROM AND WORKBOOK. ADDITIONALLY, UPON ENTERING MATERIALS ON THE CD-ROM, YOU ARE RESPONSIBLE FOR THE CONTENT OF THAT MATERIAL. FAIRCHILD HAS NO RESPONSIBILITY FOR THE CONTENT OF ANY MESSAGES OR INFORMATION POSTED BY USERS. IN NO EVENT SHALL FAIRCHILD BE LIABLE FOR YOUR LOST PROFIT OR SALES, BUSINESS INTERRUPTION OR LOSS OF DATA OR ANY DIRECT, INDIRECT, INCIDENTAL, CONSEQUENTIAL, SPECIAL OR PUNITIVE DAMAGES. NOTWITHSTANDING THE ABOVE, IN NO EVENT SHALL FAIRCHILD'S TOTAL LIABILITY TO YOU OR ANY OTHER PARTY, UNDER ANY REMEDY OR THEORY OF LAW, EXCEED THE TOTAL AMOUNT PAID TO FAIRCHILD BY YOU FOR THE USE OF THE CD-ROM.

7. Miscellaneous. You agree not to assign this agreement to any person or entity without the prior written consent of Fairchild. This agreement sets forth the entire understanding of the parties, supercedes any prior agreements with respect to the subject matter hereof, and no representations, undertakings or agreements not contained herein shall be binding on either party. This agreement will be governed by New York law without effect to any principles of conflicts of laws, and any action based on or alleging a breach of this agreement must be brought in the state or federal courts in New York.

CHAPTER ONE

Making a Profit

The most important buyer activities that affect profits are the purchasing and pricing of goods. The retail price placed on an item is influenced by many factors and normally is not an established percentage of increase over cost. This is particularly true when dealing with fashion items.[1] The four major factors that affect price are:

1. **Store/company policy.** The target markets toward which the goods in a department or store are oriented say a great deal about the price. A store's or company's target market can be profiled by age, gender, ethnicity, income, and other demographic characteristics. As the income level of the target market increases, the quality and uniqueness of an item becomes more important, and the consumer will be more willing and able to pay a higher price for these desirable characteristics. Additionally, in these stores in which prestige and quality are emphasized, prices are handled normally as round figures to differentiate from reduced or discounted merchandise. To avoid any misconceptions about the target market and to have consistent pricing, most retail stores have policies outlining the prime price ranges, zones, and lines. These policies should lead to what the store's clientele perceive as acceptable prices. A price range is defined as prices that appeal to a specific target market. Price zones are groupings of prices such as low, medium, high, promotional, volume, and prestigious. Within each price zone, there are several price lines that are the unit prices at which products are sold. There should be enough price lines to offer consumers a selection in price, however, the tendency for novices is to have too many prices that are too close together. The intervals between price lines also will become wider as prices increase.

2. **Customer acceptance.** When a fashion item is just beginning to come into vogue and is not available readily, the exclusiveness will be reflected in the price. As the fashionability of an item increases, the demand increases and the price drops as volume purchases increase. Finally, as the item loses popularity or the end of the season approaches, the price is lowered to move the remaining merchandise and to make room for the latest styles.

[1] While the word *fashion* typically is associated with apparel, other products (such as, gifts, accessories, and home furnishings) also can be trendy, and could be classified as fashion.

3. **Competition.** Without comparable prices there would be no competition. Some staple items that are always carried in stock may be priced quite low to attract consumers. However, prices that are too low create skepticism on the part of the consumer and raise questions as to the quality of the merchandise. Conversely, prices that are too high scare away consumers who are looking for the lowest possible price. Stores also can compete by offering better customer services and benefits, such as convenient store hours and location, more personalized sales attention, gift wrapping, accepting a wider range of charge cards, or offering the services of personal shoppers. When prices are comparable such services will give a business a competitive edge.

4. **Profit potential.** The sum of the prices at which all products sold in a company must cover the cost of the merchandise, operating expenses, and an additional amount that is called **profit**. The profit derived is called the profit margin and often is expressed as a percentage of net sales. The profit margin for retail operations is considerably smaller than for other forms of business due to being a very labor-intensive industry with heavy competition. The price the retailer pays for the product is called the **cost**. By such actions as purchasing in larger quantities, negotiating better terms for shipping and handling, and locating a lower-priced resource, the cost of a product can be reduced and profits increased.

Operating expenses can also be reduced to improve profit. Expense cutting measures include such actions as reducing the number of employees on the sales floor, cutting advertising costs, or using less energy by altering room temperatures. While operating expenses typically are not calculated per item, this figure must be taken into account when pricing merchandise and calculating profit. The major expense categories for a retail operation are personnel, rent, utilities, taxes, insurance, and promotion. Higher-priced products and those that are more difficult to compare in the market place typically will have more profit potential per unit because consumers cannot easily find comparable products for comparison. Items that carry a lower price and are sold in large quantities also have good profit potential due to the volume of dollars generated. The key is in pricing items high enough to cover the cost of goods, operating expenses, and profit, while still pricing it low enough to generate a good sales volume. It is possible to have a scenario in which sales volume is increased by using more advertising, but the profit margin is lowered because the related promotional expense was too costly. Expenses must be controlled to attain a profit and retailers will look for ways to cut expenses without negatively impacting business. All of these pricing considerations are part of the planning process **before** purchasing merchandise. Generally, it is best to establish a retail price while purchasing merchandise rather than waiting for the merchandise to arrive at the store.

INDIVIDUAL MARKUPS

Profit is the major goal for a retailer. A retailer's business is to supply goods to consumers. Because this service is performed with the expectation of making money, the goods must be priced so the amount of money that is received is more than the amount that is spent. The cost of the merchandise must be increased or marked up to cover such factors as operating expenses and shortages, as well as to increase the retailer's income or profit. *Equation 1.1* illustrates the markup formula for a single item, which is called the **individual markup**. Because the initial retail price of an item is derived from the cost of the merchandise and the markup, we will refer to this formula as the RCM relationship. After you know how to calculate the retail price of one item you will be able to calculate the total retail for any number of items. Additionally, after any two items in the formula are known, you will be able to calculate the third item, which is called the unknown.

Basic RCM Relationship

Dollar markup ($MU) on an item is the difference between the retail price and the cost. The **retail price** is what the customer pays for an item. For the retailer to make a profit, the price must be higher than the cost. The basic formula that describes this relationship in dollars and cents states that the dollar retail value equals the dollar cost plus the dollar markup. The basic formula is illustrated as follows:

EQUATION 1.1

$$\$Retail = \$Cost + \$Markup$$

Whenever two of the three quantities are known, you can always find the third by rewriting the equation. Consequently, the basic equation can be rewritten to find dollar cost or dollar markup. The following series of problems illustrates this point.

Problem A buyer for the Dusty Rose Specialty Shop orders a dozen sweaters for $6.50 each. She applies a $5.45 markup per sweater to cover expenses and provide a profit. What is the retail price of each sweater?

Solution
$$\$Retail = \$Cost + \$Markup$$
$$= \$6.50 + \$5.45$$
$$= \$11.95$$

Problem Ken Caulfield, a hardware store buyer, thinks that the cordless screwdriver he purchased for $14 will sell well, if marked at $32.98. What would be the dollar markup?

Solution
$$\$Markup = \$Retail - \$Cost$$
$$= \$32.98 - \$14.00$$
$$= \$18.98$$

Problem You have just taken over as the new buyer for Mountain High Cyclery and you find a cycling windbreaker that retails for $28.00. The records indicate that the markup was $14.55. How much did your predecessor pay for the item?

Solution
$$\$Cost = \$Retail - \$Markup$$
$$= \$28.00 - \$14.55$$
$$= \$13.45$$

Retail Markup Percentage

As a buyer, you will find it advantageous to look at the **retail markup percentage** (**RMU%**). Retail percentages are calculated as a percentage of net sales. The net sales figure is the sales figure that is derived after taking into account the merchandise returned to the store because it is no longer wanted or money has been given back to the customer because of a product flaw or defect. When figures are converted to percentages they can be compared on a scale from 0% to 100%. It would be unrealistic to compare the promotional costs in dollars for a fifty-store chain and an independent retailer with one store. However, by using promotional costs that are expressed as a percentage of net sales, a more equitable plane can be established on which to compare expenses between two retail operations. In both cases, the net sales figures would be 100%. The promotional costs would be expressed as a percentage of net sales.

Whenever percentages are discussed, the most important question to ask is: "Percentage of what?" In the case of markup, the markup percentage can be calculated based on retail or on cost. Most retailers now prefer to base markup percentages on the retail price. The retail percentage is used most frequently for several reasons but primarily because the inventory usually is based on retail figures. The retail method of taking inventory uses the information printed on the price tag when recording an item and its retail price. By using the retail price, inventory errors tend to be reduced.

The cost method may be used by small retailers and those that have day-to-day inventory that easily can be counted, such as a newsstand or kiosk. Departments or stores that offer such services or value-added dimensions as bakeries, candy counters, and restaurants also use the cost method because they only know the value of their raw costs.

There is an additional reason that stores prefer the retail markup percentage to the cost markup percentage. When quoting the markup percentage to customers, the lower the figure the better. The markup due to cost is always higher than the equivalent markup based on retail. In fact, the CMU% equals the ratio of the RMU% to its complement, that is, CMU% = RMU% ÷ (100% - RMU%). The CMU% can exceed 100%; whereas, the RMU% can never exceed 100%. Thus, the retailer using the retail method has a psychological advantage. The markup conversion table, *Figure 1.1*, provides a comparison of equivalent markups using the two methods.

When the cost method is used, additional work is required. For example, using the cost method, an item is assigned a cost code that is printed on the price tag; a planned markup is subtracted from every retail price; or, the cost of each item is found by searching previous records. Although inventory based on retail is a newer method than that based on cost, it is easy to see why it has been adopted readily. Retail prices also are used as the base for nationwide statistics provided by the National Retail Federation in their publication *Merchandising and Operating Results (MOR)*. The statistics present retailers with opportunities to compare their operations with other stores of comparable size. Thus, the retail markup percentage (RMU%), is referred to by many as **the** markup percentage or MU%. In this text, the term markup refers to retail markup unless stated otherwise.

When calculating markup percentage, the equation is stated as: markup divided by retail. We simply are asking the question: "What percentage of the retail price equals the markup?" If an item has a markup of $50 and retails for $100, it would have a 50% retail markup ($50 ÷ $100). A 50% markup is referred to as a **keystone markup**. Keystoning is the practice of setting the markup value at 100% of the cost. This means

FIGURE 1.1

Markup Conversion Table

RMU%	CMU%	RMU%	CMU%
5	5.26	55	122.22
10	11.11	60	150.00
15	17.65	65	185.71
20	25.00	70	233.33
25	33.33	75	300.00
30	42.86	80	400.00
35	53.85	85	566.67
40	66.67	90	900.00
45	81.82	95	1,900.00
50	100.00	100	Infinity

that the retail price is twice the cost. This is equivalent to setting the markup percentage at 50% of the retail price. This common pricing method is used by small stores because it is quick and easy. However, this pricing method does not take into account the fashionability of the product, its exclusivity, or any other considerations that would allow for more creative pricing strategies. Please note: when calculating these markup figures, it will be necessary to re-express a percentage as a decimal figure. The percent sign (%) is shorthand for "division by 100", so $35\% = 35 \div 100 = .35$.

When the retail markup percentage and dollar retail are known, the dollar markup can be calculated. These circumstances exist when the retailer has a markup goal and an established price at which the product is to be sold. The dollar markup is calculated by dividing the RMU% by 100 and multiplying by the dollar retail. This shown in the following:

EQUATION 1.2

$$\$Markup = \left(\frac{RMU\%}{100\%} \right) \$Retail$$

This is the basic equation for calculating markup percentage and can be rewritten to calculate whatever quantity is unknown, as in:

$$RMU\% = \left(\frac{\$Markup}{\$Retail} \right) 100\%$$

It also may be necessary to combine equations. For instance, if the dollar cost and dollar retail are known, we can calculate the dollar markup (see equation 1.1) to find the markup percentage, as in:

$$RMU\% = \left(\frac{\$Retail - \$Cost}{\$Retail} \right) 100\%$$

Problem A buyer from the linen department purchased decorative pillows to retail for $7.00. This department has a planned markup of 38%. What was the dollar amount of the markup?

Solution
$$\$Markup = \left(\frac{RMU\%}{100\%}\right)\$Retail$$

$$= \left(\frac{38\%}{100\%}\right)\$7.00$$

$$= (.38)\,\$7.00$$

$$= \$2.66$$

Problem Yesterday a shipment of designer scarves arrived. The assistant manager wants each scarf to have a dollar markup of $21.00. The advertised price is $37.50. What is the retail markup percentage?

Solution
$$RMU\% = \left(\frac{\$Markup}{\$Retail}\right)100\%$$

$$= \left(\frac{\$21.00}{\$37.50}\right)100\%$$

$$= (.56)\,100\%$$

$$= 56\%$$

Problem A vendor in Colorado charges you $28.90 for each of ten camping stoves. During the holiday season you plan to price them at $49.00 each. What would the retail markup percentage be?

Solution *Step 1 Use equation 1.1 to find the dollar markup.*

$$\$Markup = \$Retail - \$Cost$$

$$= \$49.00 - \$28.90$$

$$= \$20.10$$

Step 2 Use equation 1.2 to find the retail markup percentage.

$$RMU\% = \left(\frac{\$Markup}{\$Retail}\right)100\%$$

$$RMU\% = \left(\frac{\$20.10}{\$49.00}\right)100\%$$

$$= (.41)\,100\%$$

$$= 41\%$$

Problem Wigglies Bargain Basement generally plans a 44% markup on pierced earrings. Their buyer, Mr. Matthews, has just ordered a shipment. He has figured that each pair will bear a $1.43 markup. What will be the retail price of each pair?

Solution

$$\$Retail = \left(\frac{\$Markup}{RMU\%} \right) 100\%$$

$$= \left(\frac{\$1.43}{44\%} \right) 100\%$$

$$= \$3.25$$

Dollar Retail from Cost and Retail Markup Percentage

Dollar retail also can be calculated when only dollar cost and retail markup percentage are known. The dollar retail becomes the dollar cost divided by the complement of the retail markup percentage. The **complement of a percentage** is the difference between 100% and the percentage. Therefore, a percentage plus its complement will always equal 100%. For example, the complement of a MU% = 100% - MU%. The formula for calculating dollar retail from cost and retail markup percentage is:

EQUATION 1.3

$$\$Retail = \left(\frac{\$Cost}{Complement\ of\ RMU\%} \right) 100\%$$

Problem A picture frame you are selling cost you $5.20. To cover operating expenses, gross margin, and to achieve a profit, your markup must be 48%. What is the lowest price for which you can sell the picture frame?

Solution

$$\$Retail = \left(\frac{\$Cost}{Complement\ of\ RMU\%} \right) 100\%$$

$$\$Retail = \left(\frac{\$5.20}{100\% - 48\%} \right) 100\%$$

$$= \left(\frac{\$5.20}{52\%} \right) 100\%$$

$$= \$10.00$$

Dollar Cost from Retail Markup Percentage

When the retail markup percentage and the dollar retail are given, the dollar cost may be determined. The process is similar to that used in the previous section. The dollar cost becomes the dollar retail multiplied by the complement of the retail markup percentage, as in the following formula:

EQUATION 1.4

$$\$Cost = \$Retail \left(\frac{Complement\ of\ RMU\%}{100\%} \right)$$

Problem   The buyer at Todd's Togs has been very successful selling a line of warmups that retail for $36.95 each. The buyer wants to continue retailing at that price and still keep a minimum 40% retail markup. What is the highest price that a vendor could be paid for each warmup?

Solution

$$\$Cost = \$Retail\left(\frac{Complement\ of\ RMU\%}{100\%}\right)$$

$$= \$36.95\left(\frac{100\% - 40\%}{100\%}\right)$$

$$= \$36.95\ (.60)$$

$$= \$22.17$$

Problem   Suppose you are a buyer for the shoe department and want to retail a group of shoes for between $35.00 and $39.00. You have budgeted for an overall departmental retail markup of 42%. What is the highest cost bracket you could consider when buying shoes?

Solution   *Step 1* Find the highest cost for shoes retailing at $35.00.

$$\$Cost\ A = \$Retail\left(\frac{Complement\ of\ RMU\%}{100\%}\right)$$

$$= \$35.00\left(\frac{100\% - 42\%}{100\%}\right)$$

$$= \$35.00\ (.58)$$

$$= \$20.30$$

Step 2 Find the highest cost for shoes retailing at $39.00.

$$\$Cost\ B = \$39.00\left(\frac{100\% - 42\%}{100\%}\right)$$

$$= \$39.00\ (.58)$$

$$= \$22.62$$

The highest acceptable cost price would be between $20.30 and $22.62.

Cost Markup Percentage

The older method of figuring markup percentages is to base the calculations on the cost. This is referred to as the **cost markup percentage (CMU%)**. Some of the smaller stores still use this method, as well as stores that have a multitude of small items at various prices. Manufacturers also employ this method. Because the manufacturer markets merchandise to the retailer, the primary concern is not the retail price the customer pays, but rather the cost to the retailer. Once again, we are dealing with percentages. Consequently, we ask "Percent of what?" In other words, "What percentage of cost equals dollar markup?" as illustrated in the following:

EQUATION 1.5

$$CMU\% = \left(\frac{\$Markup}{\$Cost}\right)100\%$$

Problem   You are a perfume buyer for Great Sense. The planned cost markup for most discounted perfume is 28%. A vendor from New York offers you a perfume for $23.59. What would the dollar markup be?

Solution

$$\$MU = \left(\frac{CMU\%}{100\%}\right)\$Cost$$

$$= \left(\frac{28\%}{100\%}\right)\$23.59$$

$$= (.28)\,\$23.59$$

$$= \$6.61$$

Problem   Zac's costume jewelry buyer, Ms. Dodson, purchased a group of necklaces costing $18.48 each. She applied a $11.47 markup to each one. What was the cost markup percentage?

Solution

$$CMU\% = \left(\frac{\$Markup}{\$Cost}\right)100\%$$

$$= \left(\frac{\$11.47}{\$18.48}\right)100\%$$

$$= (.6207)\,100\%$$

$$= 62.07\%$$

Problem   For inventory purposes, a merchandising intern wants to know the cost of a pair of boy's slacks that have a $5.44 markup. The cost markup percentage is 34%.

Solution

$$\$Cost = \left(\frac{\$Markup}{CMU\%}\right)100\%$$

$$= \left(\frac{\$5.44}{34\%}\right)100\%$$

$$= \left(\frac{\$5.44}{.34}\right)100\%$$

$$= \$16.00$$

Additional Markup

Additional markup applies only to merchandise on hand. An additional markup is an upward revision of the original retail price. The cost remains constant because the purchase has been made and the cost of these items is settled. However, one reason for employing an additional markup is an increase in the cost of new goods. As the cost of these new goods increases, it becomes necessary to raise the retail price of items on hand to meet the standard markup. To sell both new goods being received and the items on hand at this higher price, we increase the markup of the items on hand. This dollar value is termed the additional markup. Another reason for additional markups is fluctuating market conditions. During a period of inflation, rapid price increases necessitate employing additional markups to stay ahead of rising costs. When dealing with fashion products, the salability of an item increases along with public acceptance, and if the demand exceeds the supply, consumers will be willing to pay more for the merchandise. An additional markup may be needed if the original retail price was unrealistic. A retail price can be so low that the consumer is leery of quality, durability, or serviceability. Moreover, an adjustment of the retail price may be warranted if the price is too far below the competitors and, as discussed earlier, has created skepticism on the part of the consumer.

It is important to notice that in all these scenarios involving additional markup, the cost of the items on hand remains unaffected. The additional dollar markup is the difference between the increased retail price and the previous retail price, as stated in the following formula:

EQUATION 1.6

$$Additional\ \$Markup\ =\ Increased\ \$Retail\ -\ Previous\ \$Retail$$

Problem   EMCOS has been purchasing ties for $5 each. This cost will increase to $5.50 beginning next month. To cover this increase in cost, the men's furnishings buyer is planning to increase the retail price by continuing to employ a 45% retail markup on the merchandise. At the end of the month there are 10 ties left over. These ties should be sold at the same price as the new ones that have just arrived. What is the additional markup on each of the leftover ties? (Use *equations 1.3 and 1.6* to find both retail prices.)

Solution   *Step 1* Find the increased retail price when increased cost and retail markup percentage are known. Use *equation 1.3* to find the increased retail price:

$$Increased\ \$Retail = \left(\frac{Increased\ \$Cost}{Complement\ of\ RMU\%} \right) 100\%$$

$$= \left(\frac{\$5.50}{100\% - 45\%} \right) 100\%$$

$$= \left(\frac{\$5.50}{.55} \right) 100\%$$

$$= \$10.00$$

Step 2 Find the previous retail price when the previous cost and retail markup percentage are known. Use *equation 1.3* to find the previous retail price:

$$Previous \; \$Retail = \left(\frac{Previous \; \$Cost}{Complement \; of \; RMU\%} \right) 100\%$$

$$= \left(\frac{\$5.00}{100\% - 45\%} \right) 100\%$$

$$= \left(\frac{\$5.00}{.55} \right) 100\%$$

$$= \$9.09$$

Step 3 Use *equation 1.6* to find the additional dollar markup.

$$Additional \; \$Markup = Increased \; \$Retail - Previous \; \$Retail$$

$$= \$10.00 - \$9.09$$

$$= \$.91$$

Computer Drill 1: Individual Markups

The computer drill **Individual Markups** offers you the opportunity to practice six types of markup problems, which are listed in the drop down menu located to the right of **Making a Profit**. The types of problems available are:

- *Basic RCM Relationship*
- *Retail Markup Percentage (RMU%)*
- *Dollar Markup from Cost and Retail Markup Percentage*
- *Dollar Cost from Retail Markup Percentage*
- *Cost Markup Percentage (CMU%)*
- *Additional Markup*

By selecting the overall title of the drill (in this case, Individual Markups), the program will automatically generate practice problems from the six available types of problems. To perform this type of practice, select INDIVIDUAL MARKUPS and click on the button labeled "problems." For each problem, enter the answer and choose "submit." The program will indicate whether the answer is correct or incorrect. If the answer is incorrect, you may try again and enter another answer. There is a "solution" help button available to use in the practice mode. If the answer is correct, select "next" to have the program generate another problem. You can continue in this mode for as long as you feel necessary.

Perhaps you need more practice on just one particular type of problem. You may select that problem type from the drop down menu under the overall drill title. The procedure for answering problems is the same.

Assignments

1. A buyer from Evening Encounters purchases a formal for $67.00 and applies a $48.00 markup. The item should retail for $_____?

2. If Jems and Jewels is retailing a watch for $33.00 and the markup is $12.00, then the original cost of the watch would have been $_____?

3. You are training to be an assistant buyer at a specialty store. Your buyer, Ms. Jackson, has told you that an order, which should arrive while she is gone, has a 35% retail markup. The shipment of robes has just arrived and will be given a $23.00 markup, resulting in a retail price for each robe of $_____?

4. The Bluebird Book Store is retailing a book for $44.00 and the item cost the store $24.64. This means that the store applied a retail markup of _____%?

5. The Super Sport Store is retailing a weight set for $66.50 and the item cost the store $35.00. This means that the store applied a cost markup of _____%?

6. As a buyer trainee for the Quilted Camel, you must record the retail price for sweaters costing $49.77 each. You decide to employ a 37% RMU. However, your buyer says that this type of sweater is likely to be fashionable only for a short time. She suggests adding an additional markup of $31.63. The new retail price for each sweater would be $_____?

7. The sales representative for Crazy Clocks has just told you that your new order of clocks will cost you $27.79 each instead of $20.91 each. The manager tells you that she has decided to handle the increase in cost by continuing to employ the same 49% RMU as before, thereby increasing the retail price. To retail all the clocks at the same price, the additional markup that you must add to each of the clocks that are in stock already is $_____?

8. The Nouveau Store's buyer purchased a rack of dresses for $51.66 each. To realize a retail markup of at least 37%, they each must be priced at no less than $_____ ?

9. The buyer for CoverUps purchased a rack of jackets for $67.67 each. To realize a retail markup of 33%, they must be able to retail for $_____ ?

10. A housewares buyer thinks that customers will purchase cookware sets if the retail price is no higher than $150.00. If the buyer wants to realize a retail markup of 49%, the highest dollar cost that could be considered for each set would be $_____ ?

11. The assistant buyer knows that the markup on each baby crib is $35.52 and that the store uses a cost markup of 74%. Therefore, the cost of a crib would be $_____ ?

CUMULATIVE MARKUP

As a buyer, frequently you will want to know the total markup on all the items you have purchased rather than just focusing on a single item. This total markup figure is called cumulative markup. **Cumulative markup** is the sum of all the individual markups under consideration. It is the total markup to date and does not incorporate reductions due to markdowns, shortages, or discounts. While the cumulative markup percentage may be more convenient to use, the cumulative markup in dollars must be figured before we can calculate it as a percentage.

Cumulative Dollar Markup

The **cumulative dollar markup** is the sum of individual dollar markups. However, the most convenient way to calculate this quantity is to take the difference between the total dollar retail and total dollar cost for the period under consideration. This means that the totals may include values for existing inventory, purchases to date, and any planned purchases for the period. This formula is stated simply as:

EQUATION 1.7

$$Cumulative \, \$Markup \, = \, Total \, \$Retail \, - \, Total \, \$Cost$$

Problem Karen Wheeler is assessing her department's performance over a six-month period ending next week. The records indicate that the beginning inventory, which was $2,000 at cost, is retailing for $3,750. During this period, there were additional purchases of $4,850 that retail for $7,250. Moreover, she plans to purchase $1,500 worth of goods to sell for $2,250. What is the cumulative dollar markup to date?

Solution

$$Total \, \$Cost = (At \, Cost): Beginning \, Inventory$$
$$+ \, Purchases \, to \, Date$$
$$+ \, Planned \, Purchases$$

$$= \$2,000 + \$4,850 + \$1,500$$

$$= \$8,350$$

$$Total \, \$Retail = (At \, Retail): Beginning \, Inventory$$
$$+ \, Purchases \, to \, Date$$
$$+ \, Planned \, Purchases$$

$$= \$3,750 + \$7,250 + \$2,250$$

$$= \$13,250$$

$$Cumulative \, \$Markup = Total \, \$Retail - Total \, \$Cost$$

$$= \$13,250 - \$8,350$$

$$= \$4,900$$

Cumulative markup usually refers to a period that includes a beginning inventory. The beginning inventory sometimes is called the opening inventory because it is the inventory on hand at the start of a specific period. Generally, inventory is planned by the month, so the opening inventory for one month should be the ending (or closing) inventory of the previous month. However, there are times when it is desirable to find the cumulative markup on a specific category of purchases, such as purchases to date or planned purchases, to determine if you are on track toward meeting markup goals.

Problem Records in the boy's department indicate the following purchases to date for belts:

Style Number	#Items	$Cost/Item	$Retail/Item
1025	20	$2.45	$5.00
1103	5	$2.50	$5.00
1138	10	$3.95	$8.00

What is the cumulative dollar markup on purchases to date?

Solution **Step 1** Find the total dollar retail to date.

$$Total\ \$Retail = \#Items \times \$Retail\ (style\ 1025)$$
$$+\ \#Items \times \$Retail\ (style\ 1103)$$
$$+\ \underline{\#Items \times \$Retail\ (style\ 1138)}$$

$$= 20 \times \$5.00$$
$$+\ \ 5 \times \$5.00$$
$$+\ \underline{10 \times \$8.00}$$

$$= \$100.00$$
$$+\ \$\ 25.00$$
$$+\ \underline{\$\ 80.00}$$

$$= \$205.00$$

Step 2 Find the total dollar cost to date.

$$Total\ \$Cost = \#Items \times \$Cost\ (style\ 1025)$$
$$+\ \#Items \times \$Cost\ (style\ 1103)$$
$$+\ \underline{\#Items \times \$Cost\ (style\ 1138)}$$

$$= 20 \times \$2.45$$
$$+\ \ 5 \times \$2.50$$
$$+\ \underline{10 \times \$3.95}$$

$$= \$\ 49.00$$
$$+\ \$\ 12.50$$
$$+\ \underline{\$\ 39.50}$$

$$= \$101.00$$

Step 3 Find the cumulative dollar markup for belts purchased to date.

$$Cumulative \ \$Markup \ = \ Total \ \$Retail \ - \ Total \ \$Cost$$

$$= \$205 \ - \ \$101$$

$$= \$104$$

Computer Drill 2: Cumulative Markup

If you would like to practice problems under this drill, select **Cumulative Markup** from the drop down menu to the right of Making a Profit. Since there is only one type of problem in this drill, selecting the capitalized CUMULATIVE MARKUP or the Cumulative Markup option under the overall title will yield the same functionality within the program. Remember, you have the "solution" help button if you need it.

Assignments

1. William's Department Store recently has reorganized buying areas and departments. Miss Jones now will be buying for what was previously three separate departments with related merchandise. She took an inventory of the present stock with the following results:

Department	$Cost	Present $Retail
63	$1,760.15	$2,830.00
20	$1,500.05	$2,430.00
30	$1,380.56	$2,860.00

This month she plans to purchase an estimated $2,790.87 worth of goods to sell at $4,140.00. What will be the cumulative dollar markup for Miss Jones' new, consolidated buying area?

2. A merchandise manager for the Phillip's Department Store is examining the departments in terms of their cumulative markups. Present records reveal the following:

Department	$Retail	Present $Cost
20	$679.00	$441.32
68	$882.00	$492.96

One of the buyers plans to purchase $753.00 of retail merchandise at a cost of $355.21. What will be the cumulative markup after the purchase?

3. The records for department 20 show the following purchases to date:

Date	Style #	# Items Received	Cost	Present Retail
8/2	2878	11	$617.37	$1,128.00
8/7	3003	26	$384.66	$ 578.00
8/12	7464	3	$840.30	$1,426.00
8/17	3741	7	$304.18	$ 615.00
8/22	7243	11	$734.15	$1,138.00

What is the cumulative dollar markup on purchases to date?

AVERAGE MARKUP

While it is important for you to know how to calculate markup on a single item, the markup on all items or a group of items is more important for obtaining a clear perspective of the overall markup achieved. It is not feasible or tactically desirable for all items to carry identical markups. Thus, the **average markup (AMU)** will give you a summary profile of the markup for a group of items rather than focusing on markups for single items. The four primary reasons why individual markups may vary are:

1. **Variation in cost.** Items differ in cost, and even within a given category of merchandise—such as ladies' blouses—there may be a variety of costs. The cost may vary because the items are supplied by different vendors or a given vendor may reduce charges based on quantity purchases, or increase prices for certain styles and sizes. If a retailer used the keystoning method (50% markup) on all blouses, and the cost of blouses fluctuated over time, the result would be multitudes of prices. Customers tend to find many prices in one category of merchandise confusing, especially if the difference is slight, as in $28.05, $27.89, $27.92, $27.98, $28.01. Pricing items by price point reduces confusion for the customer and facilitates inventory control and bookkeeping by having items retailed at a limited number of price points. Establishing a single retail price for a group of items also will assist a buyer in attaining the desired overall markup goal.

2. **Risk.** Some items may require different markups because the retailer risks time and money due to additional concern for care or fashionability. Fur coats require more care, better storage conditions, and tie up more inventory dollars than all-weather coats, and therefore require a higher markup. Some items involve more of a marketing risk than others because they are more fashion or fad oriented. A drastic change in style, such as from a mid-calf to a very short skirt length, signals a need for caution and higher markups until public acceptance has been secured. Basic stock items, on the other hand, have a more predictable sales record and a smaller markup may be used.

3. **Compensation for lower markups.** Higher markups are needed to compensate for lower markups. Some items are more difficult to markup because of fierce competition. Conversely, some items are not marked up at all. These are called loss leaders. Loss leaders are items priced at or below cost and often are used to attract customers. Merchandise of this type is sold at a loss to attract customers and increase sales volume. Other items in the store are marked up to offset the loss and provide profit. The price setter must be aware of legislation concerning deceptive pricing and pricing below cost. Some states have unfair trade practice acts that regulate the right of retailers to sell certain merchandise at or below cost.

4. **Competition or exclusivity.** Lower markups also may be needed to meet the competition while other items that are exclusives may be sold with a higher markup. If many other stores are carrying the same item at a lower price, a retailer needs to lower the price to compete. However, if only one retailer in town is selling an item, and that item is desirable, the markup can be higher because consumers will pay more to have the unique merchandise.

Average Markup Percentage

In larger retail operations, the **average markup percentage (AMU%)** is a goal set by higher level management. To set this goal takes experience and planning. It requires a thorough understanding of market conditions and competitors' prices and policies. Although the AMU% already may be established in a large store setting, it is a figure you should be able to determine if you are opening a store of your own or if you become a buyer for a smaller retail operation. If you are responsible for profitability, you must know how to calculate and measure the indicators of profitability. You then will be able to check whether or not the markup percentage goal was reached before your supervisor gives you the news. Additionally, you will be able to gather enough information to determine your competitors' markup goals. The calculations involve the question: "What percentage of the total retail price equals the average dollar markup?" This question is illustrated in the following formula:

EQUATION 1.8

$$AMU\% = \left(\frac{Cumulative\ \$MU}{Total\ \$\ Retail} \right) 100\%$$

Note: if you actually were performing these calculations for a period that already had transpired, you would use the net sales rather than the total dollar retail.

Problem In the problem on page 19, we found that for the six-month period ending next month, Karen Wheeler has a total dollar retail of $13,250 and a cumulative dollar markup of $4,900. What is her average markup percentage?

Solution

$$AMU\% = \left(\frac{Cumulative\ \$Markup}{Total\ \$Retail} \right) 100\%$$

$$= \left(\frac{\$4,900}{\$13,250} \right) 100\%$$

$$= (.3698)\ 100\%$$

$$= 36.98\%$$

Problem At Nero's Specialty Shop, the merchandise on hand at the beginning of the month has a retail value of $7,500. The cost value is $4,750. During the month, the buyer plans to spend $5,250 on merchandise that should retail for $8,800. Find the average markup percentage.

Solution

$$Total\ \$Retail = (At\ Retail:)\ Beginning\ Inventory$$
$$+\ Present\ Purchases$$
$$+\ Planned\ Purchases$$

$$= \$7,500 + \$0 + \$8,800$$

$$= \$16,300$$

$$Total\ \$Cost = (At\ Cost:)\ Beginning\ Inventory$$
$$+\ Present\ Purchases$$
$$+\ Planned\ Purchases$$

$$= \$4{,}750 + \$0 + \$5{,}250$$

$$= \$10{,}000$$

$$Cumulative\ Markup = Total\ \$Retail - Total\ \$Cost$$

$$= \$16{,}300 - \$10{,}000$$

$$= \$6{,}300$$

$$AMU\% = \left(\frac{Cumulative\ \$Markup}{Total\ \$Retail} \right) 100\%$$

$$= \left(\frac{\$6{,}300}{\$16{,}300} \right) 100\%$$

$$= (.3865)\ 100\%$$

$$= 38.65$$

Problem   The owner of a men's specialty shop purchased coats at $3,500 that will retail for $7,500 during the month of November. She already had coats in stock worth $3,500. These coats are retailing for $4,750. What is her average markup percentage goal for this period?

Solution   *Step 1* Find the total dollar retail.

$$Total\ \$Retail = (At\ Retail)\text{:}\ Beginning\ Inventory$$
$$+\ Purchases\ to\ Date$$

$$= \$7{,}500 + \$4{,}750$$

$$= \$12{,}250$$

Step 2 Find the total dollar cost.

$$Total\ \$Cost = (At\ Cost)\text{:}\ Beginning\ Inventory$$
$$+\ Purchases\ to\ Date$$

$$= \$3{,}500 + \$3{,}500$$

$$= \$7{,}000$$

Step 3 Find the cumulative dollar markup.

$$Cumulative\ \$Markup = Total\ \$Retail - Total\ \$Cost$$

$$= \$12{,}250 - \$7{,}000$$

$$= \$5{,}250$$

Step 4 Find average markup percentage.

$$AMU\% = \left(\frac{Cumulative\ \$Markup}{Total\ \$Retail} \right) 100\%$$

$$= \left(\frac{\$5{,}250}{\$12{,}250} \right) 100\%$$

$$= (.4286)\ 100\%$$

$$= 42.86\%$$

Complement of the Average Markup Percentage

Although *equation 1.8* may be used to find the total dollar retail or the total dollar cost, a simpler method employs a modified version of *equation 1.3* that states that the retail price equals the cost divided by the complement of the markup percentage. By using total cost and the average markup percentage we can find the total retail price, as shown in equation 1.9:

EQUATION 1.9

$$Total\ \$Retail = \left(\frac{Total\ \$Cost}{Complement\ of\ AMU\%} \right) 100\%$$

Problem Your store has been marketing electric razors successfully for $28.95. Due to increased overhead and personnel costs you have decided to use the keystone markup as your average markup percentage goal. What is the maximum total price you, as a buyer, can pay for five dozen electric razors?

Solution *Step 1* Find the total dollar retail.

$$Total\ \$Retail = (\#Items)\ \$Retail$$

$$= (5 \times 12)\ \$28.95$$

$$= (60)\ \$28.95$$

$$= \$1,737$$

Step 2 Find the total dollar cost for the five dozen razors.

$$Total\ \$Cost = \left(\frac{Complement\ of\ AMU\%}{100\%} \right) Total\ \$Retail$$

$$= \left(\frac{50\%}{100\%} \right) \$1,737$$

$$= (.50)\ \$1,737$$

$$= \$868.50$$

Problem The buyer for women's sportswear orders 100 pair of short shorts from five different vendors, which are broken down as follows:

Style Number	#Shorts	$Cost/Item
201	10	$8.05
238	45	$7.89
256	20	$7.92
281	20	$7.98
293	5	$8.01

Find the total retail value of the 100 shorts if the average markup goal is 48%.

Solution   *Step 1* Find the total dollar cost.

$$Total \ \$Cost = \#Items \times \$Cost \ (style \ 201)$$
$$+ \ \#Items \times \$Cost \ (style \ 238)$$
$$+ \ \#Items \times \$Cost \ (style \ 256)$$
$$+ \ \#Items \times \$Cost \ (style \ 281)$$
$$+ \ \underline{\#Items \times \$Cost \ (style \ 293)}$$

$$= 10 \times \$8.05$$

$$+ \ 45 \times \$7.89$$
$$+ \ 20 \times \$7.92$$
$$+ \ 20 \times \$7.98$$
$$+ \ \underline{\ 5 \times \$8.01}$$

$$= \$ \ 80.50$$

$$+ \ \$355.05$$
$$+ \ \$158.40$$
$$+ \ \$159.60$$
$$+ \ \underline{\$ \ 40.05}$$

$$= \$793.60$$

Step 2 Find the total dollar retail from *equation 1.3*.

$$Total \ \$Retail = \left(\frac{Total \ \$Cost}{Complement \ of \ AMU\%} \right) 100\%$$

$$= \left(\frac{\$793.60}{100\% - 48\%} \right) 100\%$$

$$= \left(\frac{\$793.60}{.52} \right) 100\%$$

$$= \$1,526.15$$

Average Retail Price

As mentioned previously, buyers often find it advantageous to set a single retail price on items with differing costs and/or markups. This is called the **average retail price** (**ARP**). This average is found by calculating a total dollar retail value based on the average markup percentage (see *equation 1.8*) and dividing by the number of items, as in the following formula:

EQUATION 1.10

$$ARP = \frac{Total \ \$Retail}{\# \ Items}$$

Problem Consider again the 100 pair of shorts discussed in the previous problem. We found that the total retail value was . What is the lowest price that should be put on the ticket?

Solution

$$ARP = \frac{Total\ \$Retail}{\#Items}$$

$$= \frac{\$1,526.15}{100}$$

$$= \$15.26$$

Problem A canvas bag manufacturer produces several price lines from which you have selected the following styles at the prices and quantities specified below:

Style Number	#Bags	Cost per Bag
408	30	$ 9.50
425	20	$11.50
453	10	$13.50

For what single price can you retail these canvas bags if your retail markup goal is 49%?

Solution *Step 1* Calculate the number of items.

$$= 30\ (style\ 408)\ +\ 20\ (style\ 425)\ +\ 10\ (style\ 453)$$

$$= 60$$

Step 2 Find the total cost.

$$Total\ \$Cost = \#Items \times \$Cost\ (style\ 408)$$
$$+\ \#Items \times \$Cost\ (style\ 425)$$
$$+\ \#Items \times \$Cost\ (style\ 453)$$

$$= 30 \times \$\ 9.50$$

$$+\ 20 \times \$11.50$$
$$+\ \underline{10 \times \$13.50}$$

$$= \$285.00$$

$$+\ \$230.00$$
$$+\ \underline{\$135.00}$$

$$= \$650.00$$

Step 3 Find the total retail price.

$$Total\ \$Ret. = \left(\frac{Total\ \$Cost}{Complement\ of\ AMU\%}\right)100\%$$

$$= \left(\frac{\$650.00}{100\% - 49\%}\right)100\%$$

$$= \left(\frac{\$650.00}{.51}\right)100\%$$

$$= \$1,274.51$$

Step 4 Find the retail price for each canvas bag.

$$ARP = \frac{Total\ \$Retail}{\#Items}$$

$$= \frac{\$1,274.51}{60}$$

$$= \$21.24$$

Retail Value for Balance

For a given period, a buyer may set an average markup goal and decide how much capital will be tied up in inventory. In *Chapter Five*, you will learn how to calculate an open-to-buy. The open-to-buy plan aids the retailer in setting a variety of goals, one of which is inventory level, (i.e., how much merchandise should be available for each month's sales activity). At any point in the month after money is invested in merchandise with a specified markup or retail price, the buyer can find the retail price that must be set on the balance of the investment to achieve the desired markup goal. The resulting equation may be stated as: the **retail value for the balance** equals the total retail value minus the retail value to date, as illustrated in the following:

EQUATION 1.11

$$\$Retail\ Balance\ =\ Total\ \$Retail\ -\ \$Retail\ To\ Date$$

Problem   As a buyer for the Miami-based Surf Side Specialty Shop, you plan to invest $2,880 in swimsuits for the month of January. You would like to obtain an average markup of 40%. Your first order of 75 suits, costing $15 each, results in a 45% markup. Find the retail value for the balance of the purchases.

Solution   *Step 1* Find the total dollar retail.

$$Total\ \$Ret. = \left(\frac{Total\ \$Cost}{Complement\ of\ AMU\%}\right) 100\%$$

$$= \left(\frac{\$2,880.00}{100\% - 40\%}\right) 100\%$$

$$= \frac{\$2,880.00}{.60}$$

$$= \$4,800.00$$

Step 2 Find the retail value to date.

$$\$Ret.\ to\ Date = \left(\frac{\$Cost\ to\ Date}{Complement\ of\ RMU\%} \right) 100\%$$

$$= \left(\frac{75\ (\$15)}{100\% - 45\%} \right) 100\%$$

$$= \frac{\$1,125.00}{.55}$$

$$= \$2,045.45$$

Step 3 Find the retail value for the balance.

$$\$Ret.\ Bal. = Total\ \$Retail - \$Retail\ to\ Date$$

$$= \$4,800.00 - \$2,045.45$$

$$= \$2,754.55$$

Cost for Balance

When planning for a given period, a store owner may prefer to base decisions on the total investment to be made using a stock-to-sales ratio or other financial planning tools rather than on the sales revenue to be generated. Planning based on sales alone does not take into account such factors as the cost of goods or expenses. In such an instance, the focus would be on the cost of the goods (i.e., dollars available for investment), rather than the retail price. As the period progresses and as goods are purchased, the buyer may find that a specific number of items must be added to inventory but the amount of money available is limited. To meet markup goals, either the buyer would have to settle for fewer items at a higher markup, or the buyer would have to reduce the cost of additional purchases. The situation is analogous to finding the retail value for the balance. We calculate the **cost for the balance** as the total cost minus the cost to date, as follows:

EQUATION 1.12

$$\$Cost\ Balance = Total\ \$Cost - \$Cost\ To\ Date$$

Problem   In the previous problem using *equation 1.11*, total investments were $2,880 and the initial order of 75 swimsuits cost $1,125. What is the cost for the balance?

Solution $\$Cost\ Balance = Total\ \$Cost - \$Cost\ to\ Date$

$$= \$2,880.00 - \$1,125.00$$

$$= \$1,755.00$$

Average Markup Percentage for Balance

The markup on the remaining purchases may be found by employing the basic formula for the markup percentage, and using figures that represent the balance, or what is left in the budget for a particular period. The **average markup percentage**

of the retail value for the balance of the purchases equals the difference between the retail value for the balance and the cost for the balance divided by the retail value for the balance, as is evidenced in the following:

EQUATION 1.13

$$AMU\%\ For\ Balance = \left(\frac{\$Retail\ Balance - \$Cost\ Balance}{\$Retail\ Balance} \right) 100\%$$

Problem   Consider again the problem that used *equation 1.11*. A total investment of $2,880 was involved and an initial order was placed for 75 swimsuits with a cost value of $1,125. The retail value for the balance was calculated at $2,754.55 and the cost for the balance was $1,755. What is the average markup percentage for the balance?

Solution   Find the average markup for the balance.

$$AMU\%\ for\ Bal. = \left(\frac{\$Ret.\ Bal. - \$Cost\ Bal.}{\$Ret.\ Bal.} \right) 100\%$$

$$= \left(\frac{\$2,754.55 - \$1,755.00}{\$2,754.55} \right) 100\%$$

$$= \left(\frac{\$999.55}{\$2,754.55} \right) 100\%$$

$$= (.3629)\ 100\%$$

$$= 36.29\%$$

Problem   Mr. Jaenisch, the gift department buyer, has $44,000 to spend at cost for the coming season. He has already ordered $21,500 in merchandise that will have an average markup of 44%. His departmental markup goal is 46%. What is the lowest markup he can allow if he wants to attain this goal?

Solution   *Step 1* Find the total retail value.

$$Total\ \$Ret. = \left(\frac{Total\ \$Cost}{Complement\ of\ AMU\%} \right) 100\%$$

$$= \left(\frac{\$44,000.00}{100\% - 46\%} \right) 100\%$$

$$= \frac{\$44,000.00}{.54}$$

$$= \$81,481.48$$

Step 2 Find the retail value to date.

$$\$Ret. \, to \, Date = \left(\frac{\$Cost \, to \, Date}{Complement \, of \, AMU\% \, to \, Date} \right) 100\%$$

$$= \frac{\$21,500.00}{.56}$$

$$= \$38,392.86$$

Step 3 Find the retail value on the balance.

$$\$Ret. \, Bal. = Total \, \$Ret. - \$Ret. \, to \, Date$$

$$= \$81,481.48 - \$38,392.86$$

$$= \$43,088.62$$

Step 4 Find the cost for the balance.

$$\$Cost \, Bal. = Total \, \$Cost - \$Cost \, to \, Date$$

$$= \$44,000.00 - \$21,500.00$$

$$= \$22,500.00$$

Step 5 Find the average markup for the balance.

$$AMU\% \, for \, Bal. = \left(\frac{\$Ret. \, Bal. - \$Cost \, Bal.}{\$Ret. \, Bal.} \right) 100\%$$

$$= \left(\frac{\$43,088.62 - \$22,500.00}{\$43,088.62} \right) 100\%$$

$$= \left(\frac{\$20,588.62}{\$43,088.62} \right) 100\%$$

$$= (.4778) \, 100\%$$

$$= 47.78\%$$

Problem The owner of a small home-based business plans a trip to the Merchandise Mart in Denver. He projects a sales revenue of $9,300 for the current season with an average markup goal of 38%. He has an inventory worth $2,925 at cost and $4,500 at retail. How much should he pay for the balance of his purchases and what is the markup percentage on this balance?

Solution ***Step 1*** Find the total cost planned for the period from *equation 1.4.*

$$Total \, \$Cost = \frac{Total \, \$Ret. \times Complement \, of \, AMU\%}{100\%}$$

$$= \frac{\$9,300.00 \times (100\% - 38\%)}{100\%}$$

$$= (\$9,300.00) \, .62$$

$$= \$5,766.00$$

Step 2 Find the cost for the balance.

$$\$Cost\ Bal. = Total\ \$Cost - \$Cost\ to\ Date$$

$$= \$5,766.00 - \$2,925.00$$

$$= \$2,841.00$$

Step 3 Find the retail value for the balance.

$$\$Ret.\ Bal. = Total\ \$Ret. - \$Ret.\ to\ Date$$

$$= \$9,300.00 - \$4,500.00$$

$$= \$4,800.00$$

Step 4 Find the average markup percentage for the balance of the purchases.

$$AMU\%\ for\ Bal. = \left(\frac{\$Ret.\ Bal. - \$Cost\ Bal.}{\$Ret.\ Bal.}\right) 100\%$$

$$= \left(\frac{\$4,800.00 - \$2,841.00}{\$4,800.00}\right) 100\%$$

$$= \left(\frac{\$1,959.00}{\$4,800.00}\right) 100\%$$

$$= (.4081)\ 100\%$$

$$= 40.81\%$$

Problem   You have purchased four dozen slacks at $20 for each pair and you have given them a 38% markup. The estimated total sales for the period are $2,450 and the markup goal is 43%. To attain this goal, what markup percentage should be placed on the balance?

Solution   *Step 1* Find the total dollar cost.

$$Total\ \$Cost = Total\ \$Ret. \left(\frac{Complement\ of\ AMU\%}{100\%}\right)$$

$$= \$2,450.00 \left(\frac{100\% - 43\%}{100\%}\right)$$

$$= \$2,450.00\ (.57)$$

$$= \$1,396.50$$

Step 2 Find the cost to date.

$$\$Cost\ to\ Date = (\#Items)\ Cost\ of\ Item$$

$$= (4 \times 12)\ \$20.00$$

$$= (48)\ \$20.00$$

$$= \$960.00$$

Step 3 Find the retail value to date.

$$\$Ret.\ to\ Date = \left(\frac{\$Cost\ to\ Date}{Complement\ of\ AMU\%\ to\ Date} \right) 100\%$$

$$= \left(\frac{\$960.00}{100\% - 38\%} \right) 100\%$$

$$= \frac{\$960.00}{.62}$$

$$= \$1,548.39$$

Step 4 Find the cost for the balance.

$$\$Cost\ Bal. = Total\ \$Cost - \$Cost\ to\ Date$$

$$= \$1,396.50 - \$960.00$$

$$= \$436.50$$

Step 5 Find the retail value of the balance.

$$\$Ret.\ Bal. = Total\ \$Ret. - \$Ret.\ to\ Date$$

$$= \$2,450.00 - \$1,548.39$$

$$= \$901.61$$

Step 6 Find the average markup percentage for the balance.

$$AMU\%\ for\ Bal. = \left(\frac{\$Ret.\ Bal. - \$Cost\ Bal.}{\$Ret.\ Bal.} \right) 100\%$$

$$= \left(\frac{\$901.61 - \$436.50}{\$901.61} \right) 100\%$$

$$= \left(\frac{\$465.11}{\$901.61} \right) 100\%$$

$$= (.5159)\ 100\%$$

$$= 51.59\%$$

Proportioning Costs from a Single Retail Price

In this chapter, we have talked about the desirability of employing a single retail price to avoid customer confusion and to facilitate inventory and bookkeeping. After this retail price becomes established as an expectation of the consumer for an item that is selling well, the store builds a reputation on merchandising that item at that price line. Customers who are satisfied with that price will return and it becomes a matter of goodwill to maintain the price whenever possible. Because similar items are available at differing costs, the buyer can offset a higher than average cost by buying more items at a lower than average cost and fewer items at an above average cost. The problem for the buyer is one of determining how many items to buy at each cost to achieve the desired markup for all items at this price line.

The average cost is a weighted mean (i.e., the mean figure is found by averaging costs, but a weighted mean also takes into account the proportion of each item purchased). Add the number of items at the higher price (N_H), then multiply that sum by the higher price, plus the number of items at the lower price (N_L), multiplied by the lower price. Divide by the total number of items. This is the basic form of the equation used to calculate the proportion of high priced to low priced items:

$$Average\ \$Cost = \frac{N_H(High\ \$Cost) + N_L(Low\ \$Cost)}{N_H + N_L}$$

Step 1 Multiply through by the denominator.

$$N_H(Aver.\ \$Cost) + N_L(Aver.\ \$Cost) = N_H(High\ \$Cost) + N_L(Low\ \$Cost)$$

Step 2 Arrange low cost terms on one side and high cost terms on the other.

$$N_L(Aver.\ \$Cost) - N_L(Low\ \$Cost) = N_H(High\ \$Cost) - N_H(Aver.\ \$Cost)$$

Step 3 Factor out the number of items.

$$N_L(Aver.\ \$Cost - Low\ \$Cost) = N_H(High\ \$Cost - Aver.\ \$Cost)$$

Step 4 Solve for the proportion of low to high cost items ($N_H:N_L$).

$$\frac{N_L}{N_H} = \frac{High\ \$Cost - Average\ \$Cost}{Average\ \$Cost - Low\ \$Cost}$$

This fraction, N_L/N_H, when reduced to its lowest terms, states that for every N_H item(s) purchased at the high cost, you need to purchase N_L item(s) at the lower cost. In other words, the proportion of low to high cost items is the difference between the high and average cost divided by the difference between the average and low cost.

EQUATION 1.14

$$N_L:N_H\ for\ Cost = \frac{High\ \$Cost - Average\ \$Cost}{Average\ \$Cost - Low\ \$Cost}$$

Problem The boy's department has a $5.95 price line for T-shirts. One vendor supplies them for $3.01 and another for $3.36. In what proportions must the T-shirts be purchased to attain an average markup goal of 47%?

Solution **Step 1** Find the average cost.

$$Aver.\ \$Cost = Aver.\ \$Ret. \left(\frac{Complement\ of\ AMU\%}{100\%} \right)$$

$$= \$5.95 \left(\frac{100\% - 47\%}{100\%} \right)$$

$$= \$5.95\ (.53)$$

$$= \$3.15$$

Step 2 Find the proportion of low cost to high cost items.

$$N_L{:}N_H \, for \, Cost = \frac{High \, \$Cost \, - \, Aver. \, \$Cost}{Aver. \, \$Cost \, - \, Low \, \$Cost}$$

$$= \frac{\$3.36 \, - \, \$3.15}{\$3.15 \, - \, \$3.01}$$

$$= \frac{.21}{.14}$$

$$= \frac{3}{2}$$

For every two T-shirts purchased at $3.36, three should be purchased at $3.01.

Problem 70 canvas briefcases are to be purchased from two well-known luggage manufacturers. The briefcases will retail at $32.00 each. The first manufacturer charges $14.84 while the second charges $14.63. If the average markup was 54%, how many briefcases should be purchased from each manufacturer?

Solution *Step 1* Find the average cost.

$$Aver. \, \$Cost = Aver. \, \$Ret. \left(\frac{Complement \, of \, AMU\%}{100\%} \right)$$

$$= \$32.00 \left(\frac{100\% - 54\%}{100\%} \right)$$

$$= \$32.00 \, (.46)$$

$$= \$14.72$$

Step 2 Find the proportion of low cost to high cost items for cost.

$$N_L{:}N_H \, for \, Cost = \frac{High \, \$Cost \, - \, Aver. \, \$Cost}{Aver. \, \$Cost \, - \, Low \, \$Cost}$$

$$= \frac{\$14.84 \, - \, \$14.72}{\$14.72 \, - \, \$14.63}$$

$$= \frac{.12}{.09}$$

$$= \frac{4}{3}$$

Step 3 Find how many briefcases to buy at each cost. (That is, find the multiple of $N_L + N_H$ that equals the total number of items to be purchased.)

$$(N_L + N_H) \times \, = Total \, Number \, of \, Items$$

$$(4 + 3) \times \, = 70$$

$$7 \times \, = 70$$

$$\times \, = 10$$

Therefore, the buyer should purchase 4(10) = 40 briefcases at $14.63 and 3(10) = 30 briefcases at $14.84.

Proportioning Retail Prices from a Single Cost

During times of inflation, rising costs dictate increases in retail price lines. However, if a price line has been particularly successful, a buyer may decide to retain the line and create a new, higher price line to compensate for the increase. It is not unusual for apparel buyers to purchase close-out merchandise in bulk. Close-out items represent end-of-season merchandise, items that were manufactured in too large a quantity, or those that were not appealing to retail buyers, and therefore did not sell. Close-outs are purchased at a single cost for all items in a group. In this case, the buyer must determine those items that can be placed in each existing price line. A certain percentage must go into the higher price line to balance out those going into the lower price line. The proportion of low to high retail price items is found by subtracting the average retail price from the high price line and then dividing by the difference between the average and lower retail price, as is shown in the following formula:

EQUATION 1.15

$$N_L{:}N_H \; for \; Retail \; = \; \frac{High \; \$Retail \; - \; Average \; \$Retail}{Average \; \$Retail \; - \; Low \; \$Retail}$$

Problem The Wilcott Department Store has a $68 price line for coats that has gained wide customer acceptance. The buyer who has purchased these coats for $37.50 in the past has been notified that the cost has increased by 10%. The buyer has a 45% retail markup goal. However, the buyer would like to retain her $68 line. She plans to do this by selecting some of the more fashionable coats for ticketing at $89. In what proportion should the coats be retailed to compensate for the cost increase?

Solution *Step 1* Find the cost of the new coats.

$$New \; \$Cost = Old \; \$Cost \; + \; 10\% \; (\$Cost)$$

$$= \$37.50 + .10 \, (\$37.50)$$

$$= \$37.50 + \$3.75$$

$$= \$41.25$$

Step 2 Find the average retail price.

$$Aver. \; \$Ret. = \frac{New \; \$Cost}{Complement \; of \; AMU\%}$$

$$= \frac{\$41.25}{100\% \; - \; 45\%}$$

$$= \frac{\$41.25}{.55}$$

$$= \$75.00$$

Step 3 Find the proportion of low to high retail prices.

$$N_L{:}N_H \text{ for Ret.} = \frac{High\ \$Ret.\ -\ Aver.\ \$Ret.}{Aver.\ \$Ret.\ -\ Low\ \$Ret.}$$

$$= \frac{\$89.00\ -\ \$75.00}{\$75.00\ -\ \$68.00}$$

$$= \frac{\$14.00}{\$7.00}$$

$$= \frac{2}{1}$$

For every two coats ticketed at $68 there should be one ticketed at $89.

Computer Drill 3: Average Markup

Average Markup is the name of the computer program that generates eight types of problems for this section of the text. The types of problems available are:

- *Average Markup Percentage (AMU%)*
- *Complement of the Average Markup Percentage (100%-AMU%)*
- *Average Retail Price (ARP)*
- *Retail Value for the Balance*
- *Cost for Balance*
- *Average Markup Percentage for the Balance*
- *Proportioning Costs from a Single Retail Price (NL:NH)*
- *Proportioning Retail Prices from a Single Cost (NL:NH)*

Reminder: By selecting the overall title of the drill, the program will automatically generate practice problems from the eight available types of problems. If you need more practice on just one particular type of problem you may select that problem type from the drop down menu under the overall drill title.

Assignments

1. During the month, Mrs. Wilson plans to purchase merchandise worth $4,900.00 at retail. The stock is to have an average retail markup of 46%. So far, Mrs. Wilson has purchased $630.00 to retail for $1,080.00. What is the dollar cost for the balance?

2. Taylor's Department Store is evaluating its inventory of blazers. Mr. Culp has retail stock of $1,627.00 that cost $1,000.00. To date, he has ordered $1,213.00 to retail for $1,974.00. Next month he plans to spend $1,226.00 on items that should retail for $1,995.00. Find the average markup percentage.

3. In her negotiations with different vendors, Miss Hayes was able to purchase 190 cameras. The total retail value was $23,581.82. She wants to be able to retail all the cameras for the same price. What is the lowest price for which the cameras can be sold?

4. Novelty dinnerware recently has become a big item for Benson's Department Store. The buyer was able to obtain three different styles. The order is as follows:

Style Number	#Sets	$Cost per Set
2573	50	$55.00
4416	20	$66.00
6838	50	$59.00

If the average markup goal is 37%, what is the expected total dollar retail?

5. Mrs. Ford is interested in keeping her $47.99 line of coats. The vendor that she buys from has just notified her that due to rising manufacturing costs he has to increase the old price of $28.00 by 10%. The store manager has informed her that the store must have a 39% retail markup goal. To keep her $47.99 line, she decides to take some of her more stylish coats and create a $53.99 line. In what proportion should the coats be retailed to accomplish this goal? Note: 1) reduce answer to lowest terms; 2) enter the numerator; 3) enter a decimal; 4) enter the denominator, i.e., 6.5.

6. The home furnishings department plans to spend $3,762.00 on lamps during the month. They need to obtain an average retail markup of 34%. So far, they have purchased 80 lamps at $19.00 each. On these purchases, they plan to apply a 30% markup. Find the retail value for the balance of the purchases.

7. You have been authorized to purchase $3,080.00 worth of gifts at cost. You recently returned from a trade show in Denver where you spent $1,440.00. What is your dollar cost balance?

8. The stationery department in Benson's Department Store had an opening retail inventory of $5,700.00. So far this month, it has sold $780.00 worth of retail goods. What is the dollar retail balance?

INITIAL MARKUP

When merchandise first is received into stock, it is assigned an initial markup. The difference between the first retail price placed on an article and the cost of the item commonly is referred to as the **initial markup**. Initial markup also may be referred to as markon or original markup. During the time that an item is in inventory, its markup may fluctuate. These changes in markup will be reflected in the maintained markup, which is discussed later in this chapter.

In this section, the focus is on that original markup placed on a product or group of similar items. The initial markup for a product category rarely equals the cumulative markup, because price changes will be implemented that lower the selling price. If all the items in inventory during the specified period retain their original markup, then the initial markup will equal the cumulative markup, but this is a highly unlikely scenario.

The initial markup is the difference between the first retail price placed on an article and the cost of the item. There are, however, two ways to calculate cost. One way is to include cash discounts as part of the cost of the goods and the other way is to not include cash discounts. In both methods, the cost always includes any charges for inward transportation, that is, a charge for having the goods delivered. The method used for calculating cost depends on the bookkeeping method used by the retail establishment. Cash discounts will be covered in detail in *Chapter Three*. For the purposes of this discussion, you just need to know that they are discounts given by the manufacturers to retailers as incentives for prompt or advance payment of the bill.

Initial Dollar Markup—Cash Discounts Included in Cost

The **initial dollar markup** is obtained by subtracting the cost of the merchandise from the original retail price. However, it is the definition of the cost of the merchandise that leads to different methods of calculation. In the first and most frequently used method for calculating cost, cash discounts are deducted from the invoice cost. The initial dollar markup equals the original dollar retail price minus the cost; the cost equals the invoice cost minus cash discounts plus inward transportation. This calculation is shown in the following:

EQUATION 1.16

$Initial\ \$MU = \$Retail - (\$Cost - \$Cash\ Discounts + \$Transportation)$

Problem   A piece of jewelry with an invoice of $150 arrived at Ultra Imports on September 1. Transportation costs were $2.80 and the cash discount was $4.50, but only if the bill was paid within 10 days. The bill was paid in full on September 6. The jewelry was marked for retail at a total of $300. What was the initial dollar markup?

Solution

$$Init.\ \$MU = \$Ret. - (\$Cost - \$Cash\ Dis. + \$Trans.)$$

$$= \$300.00 - (\$150.00 - \$4.50 + \$2.80)$$

$$= \$151.70$$

If a percentage figure is required, it is based on the original retail price. To calculate the initial markup percentage:

$$Initial\ MU\% = \left(\frac{Initial\ \$Markup}{Original\ \$Retail}\right)100\%$$

$$= \left(\frac{\$151.70}{\$300.00}\right)100\%$$

$$= (.5057)\ 100\%$$

$$= 50.57\%$$

Initial Dollar Markup—Cash Discounts Considered as Additional Income

In the second method for calculating initial markup, the cash discounts are considered as additional income and as such, are not deducted from the invoice cost. The reason some companies use this method is that while the buyer is responsible for negotiating cash discounts and terms, it is the bookkeeping department that is responsible for the payment of bills. The buyer does not know whether the discount was earned until notice of the transaction has occurred. The initial dollar markup still equals the original dollar retail minus cost, but in this case, the cost is defined as the invoice cost plus the inward transportation charges. When an initial markup percentage figure is required, it is based on the original retail price. The following formula illustrates this calculation:

EQUATION 1.17

$$Initial\ \$MU = \$Retail - (\$Cost + Transportation)$$

Problem   To compare the two methods, consider the problem presented in conjunction with *equation 1.16*. The dollar retail on the jewelry was $300, the dollar cost was $150, and transportation charges were $2.80. What is the initial dollar markup if cash discounts are considered additional income?

Solution
$$Initial\ \$MU = \$Retail - (\$Cost + \$Transportation)$$

$$= \$300.00 - (\$150.00 + \$2.80)$$

$$= \$147.20$$

Then, if desired:

$$Initial\ MU\% = \left(\frac{Initial\ \$MU}{Original\ \$Ret.}\right)100\%$$

$$= \left(\frac{\$147.20}{\$300.00}\right)100\%$$

$$= (.4907)\ 100\%$$

$$= 49.07\%$$

In this initial markup problem, cash discounts were not considered as part of the cost of merchandise and will be accounted for elsewhere in the bookkeeping. Compare the last two problems. The retail price was $300. When the cash discounts were included in the cost (Method I), the initial dollar markup was $151.70. When cash discounts are considered as additional income (Method II), an initial dollar markup of $147.20 is produced. Method I will always result in a higher initial dollar markup when the retail prices are identical. On the other hand, if you wish the initial dollar markup to remain stable, Method II will always produce a higher retail price and a higher cost. The next problem illustrates this principle.

Problem   The cosmetics department received an order of perfume for which it was billed $250, plus $8.50 for shipping. A $6.25 discount was earned by prompt payment of the bill. The department has a markup goal of 49%. Find the original retail price for each of the two methods of handling cash discounts.

Solution   Method I:

Step 1 Find the dollar cost.

$$\$Cost = \$Invoice\ Cost - \$Cash\ Disc. + \$Trans.$$
$$= \$250.00 - \$6.25 + \$8.50$$
$$= \$252.25$$

Step 2 Find the original retail price.

$$\$Retail = \left(\frac{\$Cost}{Complement\ of\ MU\%} \right) 100\%$$
$$= \left(\frac{\$252.25}{100\% - 49\%} \right) 100\%$$
$$= \frac{\$252.25}{.51}$$
$$= \$494.61$$

Solution   Method II:

Step 1 Find the dollar cost.

$$\$Cost = \$Invoice\ Cost + \$Trans.$$
$$= \$250.00 + \$8.50$$
$$= \$258.50$$

Step 2 Find the original retail price.

$$\$Retail = \left(\frac{\$Cost}{Complement\ of\ MU\%} \right) 100\%$$

$$= \left(\frac{\$258.50}{100\% - 49\%} \right) 100\%$$

$$= \frac{\$258.50}{.51}$$

$$= \$506.86$$

Initial Markup Percentage in Terms of Other Percentages

Although dollar amounts have been used to illustrate initial markup, for many areas of business, often it is more useful to calculate percentages for purposes of comparison. For example, management frequently will discuss business performance in terms of percentages rather than dollar figures. Initial dollar markup previously has been discussed as the difference between the original dollar retail and the cost of the merchandise. However, initial markup also can be expressed as a sum of the percentages representing operating expenses, operating profit, reductions, and alterations divided by the net sales and reduction percentages.

The percentage figures in the numerator are all based on net sales. However, the initial markup percentage is based on the original retail price. The original retail figure is derived by adding all reductions to the net sales figure, which is the base figure for comparison and is always 100%. The following shows how this formula is derived:

Step 1 Use the formula for calculating the initial markup percentage.

$$Initial\ MU\% = \left(\frac{Initial\ \$MU}{Orig.\ \$Ret.} \right) 100\%$$

Step 2 Divide both the numerator and denominator by net sales.

$$Initial\ MU\% = \left(\frac{Initial\ \$MU \div \$Net\ Sales}{Orig.\ \$Ret.\ \div\ \$Net\ Sales} \right) 100\%$$

If the initial dollar markup equals the sum of the operating expenses, operating profit, reductions, and alteration expenses, and the original retail price equals the sum of the net sales and all reductions, we get:

$$Initial\ MU\% = (\$Operating\ Expenses \div \$Net\ Sales)$$
$$+ (\$Operating\ Profit \div \$Net\ Sales)$$
$$+ (\$Reductions \div \$Net\ Sales)$$
$$+ (\$Alteration\ Expenses \div \$Net\ Sales)$$

Then, this sum is divided by:

$$(\$Net\ Sales \div \$Net\ Sales) + (\$Reductions \div \$Net\ Sales)$$

Expressing the terms in percentages gives equation 1.18, which illustrates the computation of the initial markup percentage using other percentages found on the merchandising plan:

EQUATION 1.18

$$Initial\ MU\% = \left(\frac{Oper.\ Exp.\% + Oper.\ Profit\% + Red.\% + Alt.Exp.\%}{100\% + Red.\%} \right) 100\%$$

Problem The children's department plans to use the following figures to calculate the initial markup percentage for the Christmas season:

Operating Expenses	38%	Employee Discounts	3%
Operating Profit	3%	Markdowns	5%
Alteration Expenses	1%	Shortages	2%

Find the initial markup percentage.

Solution *Step 1* Find the reduction percentage.

$$Red.\% = Emp.\ Disc.\% + MD\% + Shortage\%$$

$$= 3\% + 5\% + 2\%$$

$$= 10\%$$

Step 2 Find the initial markup percentage.

$$Initial\ MU\% = \left(\frac{Oper.\ Exp.\% + Oper.\ Profit\% + Red.\% + Alt.\ Exp.\%}{100\% + Red.\%} \right) 100\%$$

$$= \left(\frac{38\% + 3\% + 10\% + 1\%}{100\% + 10\%} \right) 100\%$$

$$= \left(\frac{52\%}{110\%} \right) 100\%$$

$$= (.4727)\ 100\%$$

$$= 47.27\%$$

Computer Drill 4: Initial Markup

Initial Markup is the name of the computer program that generates three types of problems for this section of the text. The types of problems available are:

- *Initial Dollar Markup and Markup Percentage—Cash Discounts Included in Cost*
- *Initial Dollar Markup and Markup Percentage—Cash Discounts Considered as Additional Income*
- *Initial Markup Percentage in Terms of Other Percentages*

Assignments

1. An invoice for $1,426.95 worth of linens, plus $21.40 for shipping, was received by the buyer for the Crawford Department Store. The business office informed her that the manufacturer had given them a discount of 2.5%, which they had received. Assuming that the discount is included in the cost, what should be the retail price for the shipment, if an initial markup of 37.63% is desired?

2. In Mr. Finch's department, the manager finds that the operating expenses are 25%; the operating profit is 2%; the alteration expenses are 1.50%; and the reductions are 13.50%. Find the initial markup percentage.

3. A new style of shoe has just become popular and the Burnside Department Store wants to test it. They plan to order five dozen shoes at a cost of $25.52 and retail them for $44.00 each. The manufacturer has offered a cash discount of 1.50% and charged them $15.31 for transportation. If the store considers cash discounts as additional income, what is the initial dollar markup?

4. The Coffee Clutch received a shipment of five dozen coffee makers last week costing $33.48 each. They plan to retail them for $3,240.00. They paid the bill in time to receive the 4.0% cash discount and transportation costs were $60.26. What is the initial dollar markup?

MAINTAINED MARKUP

As stated previously, the initial markup is the first markup placed on merchandise. However, due to various other factors such as additional markups, markdowns, employee discounts, and shortages, which are discussed in other sections of the book, the initial markup may be altered. The markup that results after these adjustments have been made is called the **maintained markup**. Naturally, this quantity cannot be ascertained until after the goods have been sold. The maintained markup is the markup attained over time and is a more accurate reflection of business performance, when compared to the initial markup, which is used as a preliminary planning tool. Therefore, when judging a buyer's performance, the maintained markup—rather than the initial markup—is used as a measure.

Maintained Dollar Markup

The **maintained dollar markup** is the difference between the retail price at which the goods are sold (that is, the net sales), and the cost of the merchandise. Whether or not the cost has been adjusted for the cash discounts earned depends on the policy of a given business, as explained earlier in this chapter. The maintained markup percentage is based on the net sales—the sales that actually were attained—not those that were planned. The maintained dollar markup is calculated by subtracting the dollar cost from the net sales figure, as shown in the following formula:

EQUATION 1.19

$$\textit{Maintained } \$MU = \$\textit{Net Sales} - \$\textit{Cost}$$

Problem A housewares buyer bought four dozen mixers for a total of $898.56 and retailed them for $36 each. At the end of the season, four of the mixers remained. These mixers were marked down and finally sold for $15 each. What was the maintained markup percentage?

Solution *Step 1* Find the net sales.

$$\$\textit{Net Sales} = \#\textit{Items} \times \$\textit{Sale Price (group 1)}$$
$$+ \ \#\textit{Items} \times \$\textit{Sale Price (group 2)}$$

$$= \left[(4 \times 12) - 4\right]\$36.00 + 4\,(\$15.00)$$

$$= 44\,(\$36.00) + 4\,(\$15.00)$$

$$= \$1{,}584.00 + \$60.00$$

$$= \$1{,}644.00$$

Step 2 Find the maintained dollar markup.

$$\textit{Maintained } \$MU = \$\textit{Net Sales} - \$\textit{Cost}$$

$$= \$1{,}644.00 - \$898.56$$

$$= \$745.44$$

Step 3 Find the maintained markup percentage.

$$\text{Maintained } MU\% = \left(\frac{\text{Maintained } \$MU}{\$Net\ Sales} \right) 100\%$$

$$= \left(\frac{\$745.44}{\$1,644.00} \right) 100\%$$

$$= (.4534)\ 100\%$$

$$= 45.34\%$$

Problem The effect of pilferage on profit was being analyzed in the Hopewell store. In one season, merchandise that originally cost $30,000 was retailed for $56,600. Employee discounts were $340 and markdowns totaling $2,830 were recorded. The inventory shortage was valued at $850. What was the maintained markup percentage for this period?

Solution *Step 1* Find the reductions for the period.

$$\$Reductions = \$Employee\ Discounts + \$MD + \$Shortage$$

$$= \$340.00 + \$2,830.00 + \$850.00$$

$$= \$4,020.00$$

Step 2 Find the net sales.

$$\$Net\ Sales = Original\ \$Retail - \$Reductions$$

$$= \$56,600.00 - \$4,020.00$$

$$= \$52,580.00$$

Step 3 Find the maintained dollar markup.

$$\text{Maint. } \$MU = \$Net\ Sales - \$Cost$$

$$= \$52,580.00 - \$30,000.00$$

$$= \$22,580.00$$

Step 4 Find the maintained markup percentage.

$$\text{Maintained } MU\% = \left(\frac{\text{Maintained } \$MU}{\$Net\ Sales} \right) 100\%$$

$$= \left(\frac{\$22,580.00}{\$52,580.00} \right) 100\%$$

$$= (.4294)\ 100\%$$

$$= 42.94\%$$

Maintained Markup Percentage in Terms of Other Percentages

The **maintained markup percentage (MMU%)** can be written as a function of the initial markup, reduction, and transportation percentages. If a retailer has an initial markup percentage and knows the reduction and transportation percentages, then the maintained markup figure can be calculated. Remember that reductions represent all decreases in the retail selling price (such as, employee discounts, markdowns, and shortages). The equation for maintained dollar markup is derived as follows:

Step 1 Use *equation 1.19*: Maintained $MU = $Net Sales − $Cost. Rewrite net sales in terms of the original retail price and reductions. (If transportation has not been included in the dollar cost figure, it also must be subtracted from original dollar retail.)

$$\text{Maint. } \$MU = \text{Orig. } \$Ret. - \$Red. - \$Cost - \$Trans.$$

Step 2 Substitute initial markup for the difference between the original retail price and the cost.

$$\text{Maint. } \$MU = \text{Init. } \$MU - \$Red. - \$Trans.$$

Step 3 Divide through by net sales and multiply by 100%.

$$\left(\frac{\text{Maint. } \$MU}{\$Net\ Sales}\right) 100\% = \left(\frac{\text{Init. } \$MU}{\$Net\ Sales}\right) 100\%$$

$$- \left(\frac{\$Red.}{\$Net\ Sales}\right) 100\%$$

$$- \left(\frac{\$Trans.}{\$Net\ Sales}\right) 100\%$$

Step 4 Because the initial markup percentage is based on the original retail price, multiply the initial $MU and the $Net Sales by $Retail to get the dollar retail term in the equation.

$$MMU\% = \left(\frac{\text{Init. } \$MU \times \$Ret.}{\$Net\ Sales \times \$Ret.}\right) 100\% - (Red.\%) - (Trans.\%)$$

Step 5 Rewrite the dollar retail in the numerator as the sum of net sales and reductions.

$$MMU\% = \text{Init. } MU\% \left(\frac{\$Net\ Sales + \$Red.}{\$Net\ Sales}\right) - Red.\% - Trans.\%$$

The maintained markup percentage therefore can be derived by utilizing the initial markup, reduction, and transportation percentages as shown in equation 1.20:

EQUATION 1.20

$$MMU\% = \textbf{Init. } MU\% \left(\frac{100\% + Red.\%}{100\%}\right) - Red.\% - Trans.\%$$

Problem The initial markup percentage for the hosiery department is 39% with employee discounts of 1% and markdowns of 6%. What is the maintained markup percentage?

Solution *Step 1* Find the reduction percentage.

$$Reduction\% = Employee\ Discount\% + MD\%$$

$$= 1\% + 6\%$$

$$= 7\%$$

Step 2 Find the maintained markup percentage.

$$MMU\% = Init.\ MU\%\left(\frac{100\% + Red.\%}{100\%}\right) - Red.\% - Trans.\%$$

$$= 39\%\left(\frac{100\% + 7\%}{100\%}\right) - 7\% - 0\%$$

$$= 39\%(1 + .07) - 7\%$$

$$= 39\%(1.07) - 7\%$$

$$= 41.73\% - 7\%$$

$$= 34.73\%$$

Computer Drill 5: Maintained Markup

Maintained Markup is the name of the computer program that generates two types of problems for this section of the text. The types of problems available are:

- *Maintained Markup*
- *Maintained Markup in Terms of Other Percentages*

Assignments

1. Miss Grier was concerned about profit in her suit department. During this season she had, at original retail, $38,000.00 worth of merchandise that cost her $15,960.00. She had $1,755.60 worth of markdowns, $798.00 in employee discounts, and $478.80 in inventory shortage. What was the maintained dollar markup?

2. The Passmore Department Store hopes to have an initial markup of 50%. The manager, Mr. Siler, reported that employee discounts usually run 2%, with markdowns at 11%, and stock shortages at 1%. What is the maintained markup percentage?

3. You are a buyer for Footwear Fantasies. You bought eight dozen pair of shoes for $2,701.44. During the season, you sold all but eight pair for $67.00 each. At the semi-annual clearance, the remaining shoes were put on sale for $33.50 and all were sold at this reduced price. What was the maintained markup percentage?

GROSS MARGIN

Retailers and buyers examine key financial factors to determine the health of their business. One of these factors is the gross margin, which must be large enough to cover expenses to provide a profit. **Gross margin (GM)** can be expressed either as the difference between net sales and the cost of goods sold or as the sum of the operating profit and the operating expenses. Sometimes the term gross profit is used in place of gross margin, but this is misleading because profit occurs only if the gross margin is larger than the operating expenses. In practice, it is difficult to evaluate gross margin as a dollar amount, and percentages typically are used for purposes of comparison. Consequently, after the dollar amounts have been figured, the percentages then are calculated. It is also convenient to find the gross margin by adjusting the maintained markup.

Dollar Gross Margin

The **dollar gross margin ($GM)** can be obtained from the difference between the net sales and the total cost of the merchandise. This quantity will equal the maintained dollar markup if there are no alteration expenses and no cash discounts, or if the cash discounts are included already in the cost. As in the previous cases, the percentage figure is based on net sales. The calculation for determining dollar gross margin is illustrated in the following formula:

EQUATION 1.21

$$\$GM = Maint.\ \$MU + \$Cash\ Disc.\ Earned - \$Alt.\ Exp.$$

Problem Gates Store has recorded the following figures for the season. This store always includes cash discounts as part of the cost merchandise.

Net Sales	$150,000
Invoice Cost	$ 90,000
Transportation Charges	$ 1,300
Cash Discounts	$ 2,700
Alteration Expenses	$ 3,000

Find the dollar gross margin.

Solution *Step 1* Find the maintained dollar markup.

$$Maint.\ \$MU = \$Net\ Sales - (\$Inv.\ Cost - \$C.\ Disc. + \$Trans.)$$

$$= \$150,000.00 - \$90,000.00 + \$2,700.00 - \$1,300.00$$

$$= \$61,400.00$$

Step 2 Find the dollar gross margin. (Notice that the cash discounts already have been included in the cost.)

$$\$GM = Maint.\ \$MU + \$Cash\ Disc. - \$Alt.\ Exp.$$

$$= \$61,400.00 + \$0 - \$3,000.00$$

$$= \$58,400.00$$

If the gross margin percentage was required, the basic percentage relationship would be used.

$$Gross\ Margin\% = \left(\frac{Gross\ \$Margin}{\$Net\ Sales} \right) 100\%$$

$$= \left(\frac{\$58,400}{\$150,000} \right) 100\%$$

$$= (.3893)\ 100\%$$

$$= 38.93\%$$

Gross Margin Percentage in Terms of Other Percentages

The gross margin percentage can be expressed in terms of other percentages. Because all quantities in the dollar gross margin have their percentages based on net sales, we base the equation on net sales, and divide all the factors by net sales.

$$\$GM = Maint.\ \$MU + \$Cash\ Disc. - \$Alt.\ Exp.$$

$$\frac{\$GM}{\$Net\ Sales} = \frac{Maint.\ \$MU}{\$Net\ Sales} + \frac{\$Cash\ Disc.}{\$Net\ Sales} - \frac{\$Alt.Exp.}{\$Net\ Sales}$$

The **gross margin percentage (GM%)** is equivalent to the sum of the percentages derived for maintained markup, cash discounts, and alteration expenses, as shown in equation 1.22:

EQUATION 1.22

$$GM\% = MMU\% + Cash\ Disc.\% - Alt.\ Exp.\%$$

Problem Men's furnishings has an initial markup of 38%, employee discounts of 2%, markdowns of 6%, cash discounts equal to 2%, and alteration expenses amounting to 1% of the net sales. What is the gross margin percentage?

Solution *Step 1* Find the reduction percentage.

$$Red.\% = Empl.\ Disc.\% + MD\% + Short.\%$$

$$= 2\% + 6\% + 0\%$$

$$= 8\%$$

Step 2 Find the maintained markup percentage.

$$MMU\% = Init.\ MU\% \left(\frac{100\% + Red.\%}{100\%} \right) - Red.\%$$

$$= 38\% \left(\frac{100\% + 8\%}{100\%} \right) - 8\%$$

$$= 38\%(1.08) - 8\%$$

$$= 41.04\% - 8\%$$

$$= 33.04\%$$

Step 3 Find gross margin percentage.

$$GM\% = Maint.\ MU\% + Cash\ Disc.\% - Alt.\ Exp.\%$$

$$= 33.04\% + 2\% - 1\%$$

$$= 34.04\%$$

Problem   Mrs. Hilde is preparing the annual report for the Campbell Department Store. The business office sent the following information in terms of percentage of the net sales: initial markup of 44%, cash discounts of 2.5%, employee discounts of 2%, markdowns of 13%, stock shortage of 4.0%, transportation charges of 2.5%, and alteration expenses of 1.5%. What is the gross margin percentage?

Solution   ***Step 1*** Find the reduction percentage.

$$Red.\% = Empl.\ Disc.\% + MD\% + Short.\%$$

$$= 2\% + 13\% + 4\%$$

$$= 19\%$$

Step 2 Find the maintained markup percentage using equation 1.20.

$$MMU\% = Init.\ MU\% \left(\frac{100\% + Red.\%}{100\%} \right) - Red.\% - Trans.\%$$

$$= 44\% \left(\frac{100\% + 19\%}{100\%} \right) - 19\% - 2.5\%$$

$$= 44\%\ (1.19) - 19\% - 2.5\%$$

$$= 30.86\%$$

Step 3 Find the gross margin percentage.

$$GM\% = MMU\% + Cash\ Disc.\% - Alt.\ Exp.\%$$

$$= 30.86\% + 2.5\% - 1.5\%$$

$$= 31.86\%$$

Computer Drill 6: Gross Margin

Gross Margin is the name of the computer program that generates two types of problems for this section of the text. The types of problems available are:

- *Gross Margin*
- *Gross Margin in Terms of Other Percentages*

Assignments

1. A woman with a home-based business is interested in seeing how her business is performing after one month. Her records yield the following information:

Net Sales	$568.00
Invoice Cost	$352.16
Transportation Charges	$ 10.56
Cash Discounts	$ 14.09
Alteration Expenses	$ 8.80

What is her dollar gross margin?

2. Miss Pelan is interested in seeing how her misses department is progressing. Her records yield the following information:

Net Sales	$8,637.00
Invoice Cost	$5,441.31
Transportation Charges	$ 81.62
Cash Discounts	$ 136.03
Alteration Expenses	$ 163.24

What is her gross margin percentage?

3. Mr. A. Mazing is preparing the annual report for the Merchant Department Store. The business office sent the following information in terms of percentage of the net sales: initial markup of 32%, cash discount of 2.5%, employee discounts of 6%, markdowns of 8%, stock shortage of 3.0%, transportation charges of 2.0%, and alteration expenses of 0.5%. What is the gross margin percentage?

CHAPTER TWO

Reducing the Retail Price

Pricing should be considered as much an art as a science. While there are some mathematical tools that can be helpful in decision making, there are no absolute formulas that, if applied, will lead you to a price that is always right. Prices are not static, they are dynamic and change for a variety of reasons. It is important to be able to adjust prices in a logical, timely, and profitable manner. As prices change they must be recorded and their impact must be reflected in the retail inventory figure. In this chapter, we will discuss the various techniques involved in calculating retail price reductions and illustrate how these techniques are used.

There are many reasons for reducing a retail price. As a retailer, you may use retail price reductions as a promotional device to attract customers, as an operational device to meet competition, or to remove shop-worn items from inventory. You also may use retail price reductions to correct errors in buying and selling. In practice, discounts and markdowns frequently are the two principal methods used when reducing the retail price.

EMPLOYEE AND CUSTOMER DISCOUNTS

A **discount** is a reduction of the retail price that may be given in dollars or as a percentage of the retail price. A discount reduces the retail price and may be referred to incorrectly, by some, as a markdown. Discounts commonly are given to store employees not only as a fringe benefit of their employment, but to encourage them to promote store products. In fashion outlets, management often encourages sales associates to exemplify the fashion image they are projecting. When salespeople are allowed a discount they are more likely to purchase from within the store, if price and convenience are factors.

Discounts also are given to special customers, such as frequent or high volume shoppers, or to people involved in store-related events. The discount not only creates goodwill, but can be used as an expression of appreciation for services rendered. For special promotional events, a flat discount may be given on all sales for a set period of time. If the retailer has a computer system, the discount can be taken at the point of sale (POS). The discount percentage and duration of the discount period can be programmed in the system. In this manner, the discount automatically is computed for a specified period of time and is disengaged when the sale is over.

Dollar Discount

The **dollar discount** is the difference between the previous retail price and the reduced price. The previous retail price may be the same as the original retail price, but also can be the original retail price minus a previous markdown. Therefore, the dollar discount is calculated by subtracting the lower dollar retail from the previous dollar retail. Remember that if you know two of the three terms used in the equation you can always find the third by rewriting the equation to solve for the unknown. The basic equation for calculating a dollar discount is:

EQUATION 2.1

$$\$Discount = Previous\,\$Retail - Lower\,\$Retail$$

Problem   As an employee of Griswold's Department Store, you may buy a $75 suitcase for $50. What is your dollar discount?

Solution
$$\$Discount = Previous\,\$Retail - Lower\,\$Retail$$
$$= \$75.00 - \$50.00$$
$$= \$25.00$$

Problem   An end table is being sold for $45. This price includes a $23 discount off the original retail price. What is the normal selling price of the end table?

Solution
$$Previous\,\$Retail = \$Discount + Lower\,\$Retail$$
$$= \$23.00 + \$45.00$$
$$= \$68.00$$

Problem   You have been asked to model a suit from a local store for a fashion show. Because of your participation, you are allowed a $15 discount if you are interested in purchasing it. The suit was priced at $100. How much would you have to pay?

Solution
$$Lower\,\$Retail = Previous\,\$Retail - \$Discount$$
$$= \$100.00 - \$15.00$$
$$= \$85.00$$

Discount Percentage

The **discount percentage** is a portion of the previous dollar retail price expressed as a percent. An easy way to remember the equation is to ask the following question: "What percent of the previous retail price equals the discount?" However, when calculating the dollar discount, sometimes only the previous dollar retail and discount percentage are known. When this happens, the dollar discount is derived by multiplying the discount percentage by the previous dollar retail as shown in the following formula:

EQUATION 2.2

$$\$Discount = \left(\frac{Discount\%}{100\%} \right) Previous\ \$Retail$$

Problem Preferred customers are being given a sneak preview of a new line of original lithographs. They are offered a 15% discount on all orders placed the day of the showing. How much money would you save if you placed an order for a piece of art work that normally retails for $300?

Solution

$$\$Discount = \left(\frac{Discount\%}{100\%} \right) Previous\ \$Retail$$

$$= \left(\frac{15\%}{100\%} \right) \$300.00$$

$$= \left(\frac{15}{100} \right) \$300.00$$

$$= \$45.00$$

While it is necessary sometimes to calculate the dollar discount before figuring the discount percentage, the dollar discount may be stated by the retailer on the customer coupon. The discount percentage then is calculated by dividing the dollar discount by the previous dollar retail and multiplying by 100%.

Problem An employee purchases a $55 answering machine. Due to her employee discount she paid $49.50. What discount percentage has she been given?

Solution *Step 1* Find the dollar discount.

$$\$Discount = Previous\ \$Retail - Lower\ \$Retail$$

$$= \$55.00 - \$49.50$$

$$= \$5.50$$

Step 2 Find the percent discount.

$$Discount\% = \left(\frac{\$Discount}{Previous\ \$Retail} \right) 100\%$$

$$= \left(\frac{\$5.50}{\$55.00} \right) 100\%$$

$$= (.10)\ 100\%$$

$$= 10\%$$

Complement of the Discount Percentage

When the previous dollar retail figure and the discount percentage are known, the lower dollar retail can be calculated by multiplying the previous dollar retail by the complement of the discount percentage divided by 100%. Again, the complement is 100% minus the discount percentage. Please note: by combining steps 1 and 2 of the previous problem, the equation can be found to calculate the lower retail price, given the previous retail price and the percent discount, as in the following:

$$Lower\ \$Retail = \frac{Previous\ \$Retail\ (100\% - Discount\%)}{100\%}$$

Although you can always derive the solution from the dollar discount and discount percentage equations, it helps to memorize the equation in terms of the complement of the discount percentage.

The basic equation for calculating lower dollar retail using the complement of the discount percentage is:

EQUATION 2.3

$$Lower\ \$Retail = Previous\ \$Retail \left(\frac{Complement\ of\ Discount\%}{100\%} \right)$$

Problem As a buyer in the Topp Company, you are allowed a 30% discount on all your purchases within the store. If your purchase before discount was $225 (ignoring taxes), what is the amount you will pay for the merchandise?

Solution
$$Lower\ \$Retail = Previous\ \$Retail \left(\frac{Complement\ of\ Discount\%}{100\%} \right)$$

$$= \$225.00 \left(\frac{100\% - 30\%}{100\%} \right)$$

$$= \$225.00\ (.70)$$

$$= \$157.50$$

Computer Drill 7: Employee and Customer Discounts

Employee/Customer Discounts is the name of the computer program that generates three types of problems for this section of the text. The types of problems available are:

- *Dollar Discount*
- *Discount Percentage*
- *Complement of the Discount Percentage*

Assignments

1. A special client who receives a discount on all purchases is buying a $43.00 floral arrangement but actually is charged $36.55. The discount is _____ %?

2. Klassy Keepsakes is having a clearance sale. All items in stock are reduced 20%. How much would you pay for merchandise that had an original retail price of $32.00?

3. A customer of the Artifacts Boutique receives a bill for $52.25. A special discount of 5% has been deducted from the amount due. What is the retail value of the purchase before tax is added?

MARKDOWNS

Markdowns are the most frequent means of price adjustment. A **markdown** is defined simply as a reduction of the retail price of an item. In its simplest version, the calculations are identical to those used to determine a discount. Markdowns, however, present a broader scope of reasons for price reductions. Markdowns offer the opportunity of clearing the floor of slow-moving items, those that have reached their peak demand, and items that will soon be out of season. Markdowns also are useful in the consolidation of price lines and for encouraging purchases of odd sizes or assortments. Additionally, markdowns may be taken as a promotional device. Promotional strategies are important to the retailer as a means of attracting customers. Regular merchandise may be reduced for promotional purposes or to meet or beat a competitor's price. Promotional merchandise generally is purchased with promotional strategies in mind. A loss leader, for example, is a product intended to be priced competitively to draw customers into the store. Once in the store, the merchant is hopeful that the consumer will purchase additional, regularly priced goods. Some customers may purchase an item at any price, but many customers are attracted to reduced prices or the thought of getting more for their money. To the buyer, markdowns are a way of attracting price-conscious customers.

Another reason for markdowns is to move products that have become shopworn. While proper handling of merchandise in the store can keep it looking good and retain its value, some wear and tear is inevitable. For example, the most obvious manipulation of apparel items is while customers are examining or trying them on. Many times, buttons come off and are lost, zippers are broken, or garments are ripped or damaged in some small way. Additionally, when garments are used in window and store displays, they undergo more handling, exposure to sunlight, and sometimes unusual manipulation to fit the mannequin or the scene depicted. Garments that are transferred between departments or stores and those that are used for fashion shows also are more vulnerable to damage and soiling. Overabused garments, as well as those with flaws, are sold most easily when price reductions occur.

Having appropriate and profit-producing merchandising of most goods requires having the item in the right place at the right time. Products that are introduced prematurely to the market may meet a public that is not yet ready to accept them. When merchandise does not move rapidly, markdowns must be taken to increase movement. Those items that are introduced late in the season, because of a lack of buyer foresight in stipulating a shipping date, will not move rapidly and markdowns may be taken to sell the merchandise. Buying and merchandising errors also can cause some markdowns. The buyer who orders goods because of a personal preference or because the merchandise manager encourages the purchase, and not because of knowledge of the clientele's needs and wants, is asking for increased markdowns.

Although it is true that markdowns indicate a reduction in the markup percentage, and thus a possible reduction in revenue, it is important to reflect on what may happen if such reductions did not occur. Some items would never be sold, would take up room on the selling floor, and tie up capital needlessly. Markdowns are also a means of telling whether or not old merchandise is being removed from stock to make room for the incoming fresh stock. Thus, moving items for a lower markup percentage than originally anticipated may be much more profitable than not moving the goods at all. With the added benefit of computer technology, we easily can track merchandise based on the length of time it has been in inventory, the number of times it has been marked down, or to rate performance based on any other set of variables defined by management.

Dollar Markdown

Dollar markdown ($MD) is the difference between the retail price and the reduced price. The equation is similar to that for dollar discount. Again, we remind you that if you know two of the three variables you can always find the third by rearranging terms. The dollar markdown is derived by subtracting the lower dollar retail from the previous dollar retail, as is shown in the following formula:

EQUATION 2.4

$$\$MD = Previous\ \$Retail - Lower\ \$Retail$$

Problem If a buyer reduces a $35 tape recorder to $25, what is the markdown in dollars?

Solution
$$\$MD = Previous\ \$Retail - Lower\ \$Retail$$
$$= \$35.00 - \$25.00$$
$$= \$10.00$$

Problem A belt that regularly sells for $23.95 is reduced by $4. What is the new retail price?

Solution
$$Lower\ \$Retail = Previous\ \$Retail - \$MD$$
$$= \$23.95 - \$4.00$$
$$= \$19.95$$

Problem An ad reads "Fantastic Sale—All Tops $2 Off!" If the top you select now sells for $4, what was the previous retail price?

Solution
$$Previous\ \$Retail = Lower\ \$Retail + \$MD$$
$$= \$4.00 + \$2.00$$
$$= \$6.00$$

Problem A buyer finds that 24 calculators priced at $39.99 each are selling slowly. If they were reduced to $34.99 each, what is the dollar markdown for each calculator?

Solution
$$\$MD = \$Retail - Lower\ \$Retail$$
$$= \$39.99 - \$34.99$$
$$= \$5.00$$

Retail Markdown Percentage

When you want to know what portion of the previous retail price comprises the mark-down, calculate the **retail markdown percentage** (**RMD %**). The relationship is similar to the one for discount percentage (see *equation 2.2*). The markdown percentage is one of the most commonly used formulas by retailers and consumers. When sale merchandise signage notes "x% off," the percentage has been derived by using the retail markdown percentage formula, which is calculated by dividing the dollar amount of the markdown by the dollar retail. This is demonstrated in the following:

EQUATION 2.5

$$RMD\% = \left(\frac{\$MD}{Previous\ \$Retail} \right) 100\%$$

Problem   A luggage buyer notices that a single shopworn briefcase, which retails for $32, has been in stock for over a year. She reduces the price by $14.40 hoping to make a quick sale. What is the retail markdown percentage?

Solution

$$RMD\% = \left(\frac{\$MD}{Previous\ \$Retail} \right) 100\%$$

$$= \left(\frac{\$14.40}{\$32.00} \right) 100\%$$

$$= (.45)\ 100\%$$

$$= 45\%$$

Problem   An odd-sized slipcover is reduced 25% of the $16 retail price. How much has the price been reduced in dollars?

Solution

$$\$MD = \left(\frac{RMD\%}{100\%} \right) Previous\ \$Retail$$

$$= \left(\frac{25\%}{100\%} \right) \$16.00$$

$$= (.25)\ \$16.00$$

$$= \$4.00$$

Problem   During a 20% off promotional sale, a cardigan was marked down $3.50. What was the original price of the cardigan?

Solution

$$Previous\ \$Retail = \left(\frac{\$MD}{RMD\%}\right)100\%$$

$$= \left(\frac{\$3.50}{20\%}\right)100\%$$

$$= \left(\frac{\$3.50}{.20}\right)100\%$$

$$= \$17.50$$

Complement of the Retail Markdown Percentage

The complement of the retail markdown percentage is derived by subtracting the markdown percentage from 100%. In various formulas you have seen the word complement used interchangeably with 100% minus the number for which you are finding the complement. Just as you memorized multiplication tables when you were young, it is useful and time-saving to memorize some formulas in the text. However, just in case your memory fails, the lower dollar retail can be written as:

$$Lower\ \$Retail = Previous\ \$Retail - \$MD$$

Dollar markdown also can be written as:

$$\$MD = \left(\frac{RMD\%}{100\%}\right)\ Previous\ \$Retail$$

Therefore, the lower dollar retail can be written as:

$$Lower\ \$Retail = Previous\ \$Retail\left(\frac{100\% - RMD\%}{100\%}\right)$$

EQUATION 2.6

$$Lower\ \$Retail = Previous\ \$Retail\left(\frac{Complement\ of\ RMD\%}{100\%}\right)$$

Problem
During the annual January clearance, the Cummings Company advertises a "20% off" sale. The buyer in the men's department has an outdated sportcoat he wants to include in the sale. The sportcoat currently carries a price tag of $89. What price should be put on the sale tag?

Solution

$$Lower\ \$Retail = Previous\ \$Retail\left(\frac{100\% - RMD\%}{100\%}\right)$$

$$= \$89.00\left(\frac{100\% - 20\%}{100\%}\right)$$

$$= \$89.00\left(\frac{80\%}{100\%}\right)$$

$$= \$71.20$$

Gross Dollar Markdown

As you know, the word gross has multiple meanings. In a merchandising setting, gross is used most frequently to mean twelve dozen of some article—12 × 12 or 144. It also can be used to mean the whole or bulk of something. **Gross dollar markdown (Gross $MD)** is used to mean all of the dollar markdown, not just the markdown on one item nor just the markdown on items that were sold, but rather the total markdown for all items whether they are sold or not. To calculate gross dollar markdown, we multiply the number of items by the amount of markdown. If there is more than one group of items, we find this product for each group and then add all the products together, as illustrated in the following formula:

EQUATION 2.7

$$Gross\ \$MD\ =\ (\#Items)\ (\$MD)\ [Group\ 1]\ +\ (\#Items)\ (\$MD)\ [Group\ 2]\ +\ etc.$$

Problem In the section involving dollar markdown, a buyer found that 24 calculators priced at $39.99 each were selling slowly. We showed that if the calculators were reduced to $34.99, the dollar markdown for each was $5. What would be the gross dollar markdown?

Solution
$$Gross\ \$MD\ =\ (\#Items)\ \$MD$$
$$=\ (24)\ \$5.00$$
$$=\ \$120.00$$

Problem A buyer in the sportswear department reduced the following items: eight skirts, ten cardigans, twelve blouses, and three pullovers. The skirts were reduced $5 each; the cardigans, $3.50 each; the blouses, $2 each; and the pullovers, $1.50 each. What was the gross dollar markdown?

Solution
$$Gross\ \$MD\ =\ \#Items\ \times\ \$MD$$
$$+\ \#Items\ \times\ \$MD$$
$$+\ \#Items\ \times\ \$MD$$
$$+\ \underline{\#Items\ \times\ \$MD}$$

$$=\ 8\ \times\ \$5.00$$
$$+\ 10\ \times\ \$3.50$$
$$+\ 12\ \times\ \$2.00$$
$$+\ \underline{\ 3\ \times\ \$1.50}$$

$$=\ \$40.00$$
$$+\ \$35.00$$
$$+\ \$24.00$$
$$+\ \underline{\$\ 4.50}$$

$$=\ \$103.50$$

Problem A footwear buyer plans to reduce nine pair of sandals that retail for $25 to $18 each. He also plans to reduce twenty pair of canvas shoes from $7.95 to $4.95 each. Previously, he reduced six pair of slippers from $9.89 to $6.39 each. What was his gross dollar markdown?

Solution

$$Gross\ \$MD = \#Items \times \$MD$$
$$+ \#Items \times \$MD$$
$$+ \#Items \times \$MD$$

(Note: remember that $\$MD$ = Previous $Retail − Lower $Retail)

$$Gross\ \$MD = 9\ (\$25.00 − \$18.00)$$
$$+ 20\ (\$7.95 − \$4.95)$$
$$+ \underline{6\ (\$9.89 − \$6.39)}$$

$$= 9\ (\$7.00)$$
$$+ 20\ (\$3.00)$$
$$+ \underline{6\ (\$3.50)}$$

$$= \$63.00$$
$$+ \$60.00$$
$$+ \underline{\$21.00}$$

$$= \$144.00$$

Gross Markdown Percentage

Because the gross markdown does not take net sales into account, the **gross markdown percentage (GMD%)** is calculated as a portion of the total or gross retail dollars. In other words, what percent of the gross retail dollars equals the gross dollar markdown? This figure may be used in cases where the net sales or the actual markdown figure are not known, but the gross figures are available. The gross markdown percentage is found by dividing the gross dollar markdown by the previous gross dollar retail multiplied by 100%, as follows:

EQUATION 2.8

$$GMD\% = \left(\frac{Gross\ \$MD}{Previous\ Gross\ \$Retail} \right) 100\%$$

Problem For the month of July, the bedding department had a gross dollar markdown of $1,836 on goods retailing at $10,800. What was the gross markdown percentage?

Solution
$$GMD\% = \left(\frac{Gross\ \$MD}{Previous\ Gross\ \$Retail} \right) 100\%$$

$$= \left(\frac{\$1,836.00}{\$10,800.00} \right) 100\%$$

$$= (.17)\ 100\%$$

$$= 17\%$$

Problem The toy department recorded $3,820 in gross retail sales for the month of September with a 27% gross markdown. What was the gross dollar markdown?

Solution
$$Gross\ \$MD = \left(\frac{GMD\%}{100\%} \right) Previous\ Gross\ \$Retail$$

$$= \left(\frac{27\%}{100\%} \right) \$3,820.00$$

$$= (.27)\ \$3,820.00$$

$$= \$1,031.40$$

Problem The owners of "The Attic Bears" figured they had a total of $5,949 in markdowns for the month of March. Using an 18% gross markdown percentage, calculate the gross retail for the month.

Solution
$$Previous\ Gross\ \$Retail = \left(\frac{Gross\ \$MD}{GMD\%} \right) 100\%$$

$$= \left(\frac{\$5,949.00}{.18} \right) 100\%$$

$$= \$33,050.00$$

Problem A handbag buyer recorded the following transactions for the month of April:

#Items	Original Retail Price	Markdown
4	$25.00	$5.50
6	$18.00	$6.00
10	$14.85	$8.46

What was the gross markdown percentage?

Solution $\quad GMD\% = \left(\dfrac{Gross\ \$MD}{Previous\ Gross\ \$Retail}\right)100\%$

$= \left(\dfrac{[(\#Items \times \$MD) + (\#Items \times \$MD) + (\#Items \times \$MD)]}{[(\#Items \times \$Ret.) + (\#Items \times \$Ret.)] + (\#Items \times \$Ret.)]}\right)100\%$

$= \left(\dfrac{[4(\$5.50) + 6(\$6.00) + 10(\$8.46)]}{[4(\$25.00) + 6(\$18.00) + 10(\$14.85)]}\right)100\%$

$= \left(\dfrac{[\$22.00 + \$36.00 + \$84.60]}{[\$100.00 + \$108.00 + \$148.50]}\right)100\%$

$= \left(\dfrac{\$142.60}{\$356.50}\right)100\%$

$= (.40)\,100\%$

$= 40\%$

Problem A buyer in the infant department reduced two layettes from $74 to $60.33 each; six diaper bags from $14 to $12 each; and ten carriage blankets from $6.47 to $4.47 each. What was the gross markdown percentage?

Solution $\quad GMD\% = \left(\dfrac{Gross\ \$MD}{Previous\ Gross\ \$Ret.}\right)100\%$

$= \left(\dfrac{[(\#Items \times \$MD) + (\#Items \times \$MD) + (\#Items \times \$MD)]}{[(\#Items \times \$Ret.) + (\#Items \times \$Ret.) + (\#Items \times \$Ret.)]}\right)100\%$

(Remember: $MD = Previous $Retail − Lower $Retail)

$GMD\% = \left(\dfrac{[2(\$74.00 - \$60.33) + 6(\$14.00 - \$12.00) + 10(\$6.47 - \$4.47)]}{[2(\$74.00) + 6(\$14.00) + 10(\$6.47)]}\right)100\%$

$= \left(\dfrac{[2(\$13.67) + 6(\$2.00) + 10(\$2.00)]}{[2(\$74.00) + 6(\$14.00) + 10(\$6.47)]}\right)100\%$

$= \left(\dfrac{[\$27.34 + \$12.00 + \$20.00]}{[\$148.00 + \$84.00 + \$64.70]}\right)100\%$

$= \left(\dfrac{\$59.34}{\$296.70}\right)100\%$

$= (.20)\,100\%$

$= 20\%$

Dollar Markdown Cancellation

At the end of a sale, a buyer must decide what is to be done with remaining merchandise. There are several options. The items could be returned to their original price or repriced a little below the original retail value. The price also could be raised higher than the original price. Moreover, the unsold goods could be left at the sale price, reduced further and finally, if the items remain unsold, they can be donated to charity. In this section, we are interested in the scenario in which the markdown is canceled completely. In other words, the price of the items are raised to the original retail value. This is called **dollar markdown cancellation ($MD Cancellation)**. The equation for dollar markdown cancellation is similar to the one for gross dollar markdown (see *equation 2.7*), except that for each group, the number of items becomes the number remaining in that group. The dollar markdown cancellation is very useful when calculating the net dollar markdown (to be discussed in the next section). The dollar markdown cancellation is computed by multiplying the number of items remaining in a group by the dollar markdown per item. The sum for all groups involved in the markdown cancellation is the dollar markdown cancellation figure, as shown in the following formula:

EQUATION 2.9

$$\$MD\ Cancellation = (\#Items\ Remaining)\ (\$MD)\ [Group\ 1]$$
$$+\ (\#Items\ Remaining)\ (\$MD)\ [Group\ 2]$$
$$+\ etc.$$

Problem   After the annual back-to-school sale, the children's department canceled the $1.50 markdown on the ten T-shirts that were left. They also raised the price of each of the two dozen unsold jeans by $3, which returned them to their regular retail value. What was the markdown cancellation?

Solution

$\$MD\ Cancellation = (\#Items\ Remaining \times \$MD) + (\#Items\ Remaining \times \$MD)$

$= (10 \times \$1.50) + (24 \times \$3.00)$

$= \$15.00 + \$72.00$

$= \$87.00$

Problem   For three days only, spring plants were selling for $5.98. After the special was over, the five plants that were left were returned to their regular price of $7.98. What was the markdown cancellation?

Solution

$\$MD\ Cancellation = \#Items\ Remaining \times \$MD$

$= \#Items\ Remaining \times (Previous\ \$Retail - Lower\ \$Retail)$

$= 5\ (\$7.98 - \$5.98)$

$= 5\ (\$2.00)$

$= \$10.00$

Net Dollar Markdown

As we have indicated in the previous section, the markdown cancellation is very useful for calculating the net dollar markdown. What you really want to know after a sale is the end result, or net effect, of the markdown. Thus, the

net dollar markdown (Net $MD) is the difference between the gross dollar markdown and the dollar markdown cancellation, as demonstrated in the following:

EQUATION 2.10

$$Net\ \$MD\ =\ Gross\ \$MD\ -\ \$MD\ Cancellation$$

Problem In planning the July clearance sale the Hodgekiss Furniture Store planned a gross markdown of $6,370. After the sale, the markdown cancellation was $2,150. What was the net dollar markdown?

Solution $$Net\ \$MD\ =\ Gross\ \$MD\ -\ \$MD\ Cancellation$$

$$=\ \$6,370.00\ -\ \$2,150.00$$

$$=\ \$4,220.00$$

We have discussed several types of markdown problems separately. We are now ready to illustrate how several types can be combined to solve one large problem. Starting only with very basic information, we proceed to calculate the net dollar markdown in the following problem:

Problem Your blanket vendor announces a nationwide advertising campaign to promote pure wool blankets at 40% off the original price. You have 72 regular quality blankets that retail at $38.50 each and 18 superior quality blankets that retail for $45 each. During the advertising campaign, you sell 67 of the regular blankets and 10 of the superior blankets. The unsold blankets are returned to the original price. What was the net dollar markdown?

Solution Begin by writing down what you know. Use *equation 2.10*:

$$Net\ \$MD\ =\ Gross\ \$MD\ -\ \$MD\ Cancellation$$

Because none of these quantities are given, work back another step, by using the formula for gross dollar markdown, *equation 2.7*:

$$Gross\ \$MD\ =\ (\#Items\ \times\ \$MD)\ +\ (\#Items\ \times\ \$MD)$$

We know the number of items in each group but we need to find the dollar markdown. Consequently, we go back a step further and use the formula for calculating dollar markdown.

Step 1 Find the dollar markdown for the regular blankets.

$$\$MD\ Regular\ =\ \left(\frac{RMD\%}{100\%}\right)Previous\ \$Retail$$

$$=\ \left(\frac{40\%}{100\%}\right)\$38.50$$

$$=\ (.40)\ \$38.50$$

$$=\ \$15.40$$

Step 2 Find the dollar markdown for the superior blankets.

$$\$MD\ Superior = \left(\frac{RMD\%}{100\%}\right) Previous\ \$Retail$$

$$= \left(\frac{40\%}{100\%}\right) \$45.00$$

$$= (.40)\ \$45.00$$

$$= \$18.00$$

Step 3 Find the gross dollar markdown.

$$Gross\ \$MD = (\#Items \times \$MD) + (\#Items \times \$MD)$$

$$= (72 \times \$15.40) + (18 \times \$18.00)$$

$$= \$1,108.80 + \$324.00$$

$$= \$1,432.80$$

Step 4 Find the dollar markdown cancellation.

$$\$MD\ Cancellation = (\#Remaining \times \$MD) + (\#Remaining \times \$MD)$$

$$= (72 - 67)\,\$15.40 + (18 - 10)\,\$18.00$$

$$= (5 \times \$15.40) + (8 \times \$18.00)$$

$$= \$77.00 + \$144.00$$

$$= \$221.00$$

Step 5 Calculate the net dollar markdown.

$$Net\ \$MD = Gross\ \$MD - \$MD\ Cancellation$$

$$= \$1,432.80 - \$221.00$$

$$= \$1,211.80$$

Net Markdown Percentage

Markdowns frequently are expressed as a percentage of net sales. This technique provides the buyer with a means of comparison among other departments and other stores. When figuring the **net markdown percentage** (**Net MD%**), the salient question is "What portion of the net sales is due to the net dollar markdown?" This concept is illustrated in the following:

EQUATION 2.11

$$Net\ MD\% = \left(\frac{Net\ \$MD}{Net\ \$Sales}\right) 100\%$$

Problem   Last month the net sales for your department were $5,500. The retail value was $8,640, while the markdowns amounted to $247.50. What was the net markdown percentage?

Solution

$$Net\ MD\% = \left(\frac{Net\ \$MD}{Net\ \$Sales}\right) 100\%$$

$$= \left(\frac{\$247.50}{\$5,500.00}\right) 100\%$$

$$= (.045)\ 100\%$$

$$= 4.5\%$$

Problem   Gloves that normally sell for $15.75 a pair are on sale for $12.25. At the close of the sale one and a half dozen of the original five dozen pair remain. These are returned to their original price. What is the markdown percentage of the net sales?

Solution   Working backwards, find the net markdown percentage of net sales.

$$Net\ \$MD\% = \left(\frac{Net\ \$MD}{Net\ \$Sales}\right) 100\%$$

First, find the net $MD.

$$Net\ \$MD = (\#Sold)\ \$MD$$

Second, find the dollar markdown.

$$\$MD = Previous\ \$Retail - Lower\ \$Retail$$

Step 1   Find dollar markdowns.

$$\$MD = Previous\ \$Retail - Lower\ \$Retail$$

$$= \$15.75 - \$12.25$$

$$= \$3.50$$

Step 2   Find the number sold.

$$\#Sold = Total\ \#Items - \#Remaining$$

$$= (5)\ 12 - (1.5)\ 12$$

$$= 60 - 18$$

$$= 42$$

Step 3   Find the net dollar markdown.

$$Net\ \$MD = (\#Sold)\ \$MD$$

$$= (42)\ \$3.50$$

$$= \$147.00$$

Step 4 Find the net sales.

$$Net\ Sales = (\#Sold)\ Lower\ \$Retail$$

$$= (42)\ \$12.25$$

$$= \$514.50$$

Step 5 Find the net markdown percentage.

$$Net\ MD\% = \left(\frac{Net\ \$MD}{Net\ \$Sales} \right) 100\%$$

$$= \left(\frac{\$147.00}{\$514.50} \right) 100\%$$

$$= (.2857)\ 100\%$$

$$= 28.57\%$$

Computer Drill 8: Markdowns

Markdowns is the name of the computer program that generates eight types of problems for this section of the text. The types of problems available are:

- *Dollar Markdown*
- *Retail Markdown Percentage*
- *Complement of the Retail Markdown Percentage*
- *Gross Dollar Markdown*
- *Gross Markdown Percentage*
- *Dollar Markdown Cancellation*
- *Net Dollar Markdown*
- *Net Markdown Percentage*

Assignments

1. Idaho Pottery, Inc., has eleven ceramic vases retailing for a total of $55.00. The group of items is reduced $33.00. What is the retail markdown for each vase?

2. If a product is reduced from a single unit retail price of $57.00 to a lower retail price of $39.00, then the dollar markdown is $_____?

3. If 35 items are each reduced from a retail price of $83.00 to a markdown retail price of $66.00, then the gross dollar markdown on the goods is $_____?

4. The following are price changes in the Haeger Department Store:

Item	Number	Original Retail	Markdown Price
A	7	$11.00	$ 6.00
B	3	$86.00	$68.00
C	3	$17.00	$10.00
D	8	$16.00	$ 9.00

The gross dollar markdown for these items is $_____?

5. For the month of June, the stationary department had net sales of $3,000.00 and markdowns of $210.00. What was the markdown percentage for June?

6. If your department has monthly retail sales amounting to $7,300.00 and you have taken markdowns amounting to $803.00 during the month, then your markdown percentage for the period is _____ %?

7. The Paragon Specialty Store bought 28 handbags to sell at $86.00 each. The handbags cost $51.57 each. 16 were sold at the original retail price. Seven were each marked down $12.90 from the original price and the remainder were marked down an additional $9.00 each before they finally were sold. The gross markdown percentage for the purchase was _____ %?

8. The buyer for Durango Leather Goods takes the following markdowns during the month of June:

#Items	Original Retail Price	Lower Retail Price
3	$132.00	$113.52
2	$150.00	$139.50
8	$ 15.00	$ 14.25

Sales for June amounted to $9,600.00. What was the gross markdown percentage?

9. You are having a special promotion. In one classification, 25 items were marked down to $29.00 each. 14 items were not sold and were returned to their original price. The total markdown cancellation was $182.00. What was the original retail price per item?

10. The Lazy Leopard opened a new branch store and ran an ad in the local paper for a "2 for 1" sale. 36 lounging outfits that regularly sold for $77.00 each would now sell for $38.50. After the promotion, fifteen outfits remained and were returned to their original retail price. What was the amount of the markdown cancellation?

11. After a sale you receive the following information:
    The number of items available for the sale was 44.
    The number of items that remained after the sale was 5.
    The original retail price per item was $73.00.
    The markdown retail price per item was $58.00.
    The remaining items are returned to $73.00 each.
    The net dollar markdown would be $_____?

12. The Mad Hatter has 42 hats in stock that will have to be marked for quick clearance. 20 had retailed for $41.00 each and 22 for $29.00. The first group were reduced $6.15 each and the rest $4.35 each. If all the hats were sold, what was the net markdown percentage?

13. Ski Traders has 50 pair of goggles in stock that will have to be marked for quick clearance. 23 had retailed for $17.00 each and 27 for $11.00 each. The first group were reduced $2.55 each and the rest $1.65 each. If all the goggles were sold, what was the net markdown percentage?

14. The Image, Inc. has 16 decorative art pieces in stock that will have to be marked for clearance. Seven had retailed for $136.00 each and nine for $119.00 each. The first group was reduced $9.52 each and the rest $8.33 each. If all the pieces were sold, what was the net markdown percentage?

CHAPTER THREE

Discounts, Terms, and Datings

One of the most important aspects of a buyer's job is negotiating with vendors. This negotiation process provides the opportunity to discuss the terms of sale. This process begins after the buyer has shopped the market and found the type and quality of merchandise their customers desire. After locating the appropriate merchandise, which carries a quoted list price, the process of bargaining begins.

The buyer wants to purchase the merchandise at the lowest possible cost to maximize the store's profit objectives. The vendor wants to sell at the highest price, for the same reason. In negotiating the price of the goods, the buyer considers the selection as a whole and does not try to haggle over every item. Merchandise needed for a special promotion or sale would have to be bought at a lower cost. Consideration is always given to getting the cost low enough to meet the department or store's average markup goal. Positive buyer-vendor relations should be nurtured, which promote mutually beneficial outcomes. Neither party should expect unreasonable concessions and both must negotiate in good faith.

The price of the goods (that is, the cost billed on the **invoice**) is only one of several terms of sale that may be negotiated to reduce the total cost of the merchandise. These terms involve such variables as payment of transportation charges, provision of vendor aids, and discounts. A discount is a percentage of the price that is deducted from the list or billed cost of the merchandise. This section will discuss terms, dating, and four of the most widely used types of discounts: cash, anticipation, quantity, and trade. If all of these discounts were utilized, trade discounts would be taken first, then quantity, and finally, anticipation and the cash discount. The cash discount is always taken last, but because it is utilized in a number of different scenarios, we will examine it first.

CASH DISCOUNTS

Cash discounts are granted when the invoice is paid within a specified period. The term is somewhat misleading because it makes no difference whether or not the bill was paid in cash. They are so-called because when cash discounts are given, the amount of savings can be substantial. Consider a transaction where the net amount is due in 50 days and an 8% cash discount will be granted if the bill is paid within 10 days. A retailer who does not take advantage of the discount would in effect be paying 8% interest for the use of the money for 50 days. If the bill was not paid within the net payment period, the amount due could be subject to interest charges and could further damage the retailer's credit rating. However, if partial payment is made on the amount due within the discount period, the buyer should be granted a discount on the portion of the bill that is paid.

Cash Discounts and Other Terms of Sale

Cash discounts normally are written as part of the terms of sale and should be discussed with the vendor beforehand and recorded on the order. Terms have many variations and are presented in different ways. The following variations will be discussed: regular dating, receipt of goods dating (ROG), end of month dating (EOM), and extra dating. These terms have three main components: discount, duration, and date due. For instance, 2/10, net 30 on an invoice means that if this bill was paid within 10 days of the date of the invoice, the retailer would be granted a 2% cash discount. In any case, the net amount must be paid within 30 days.

The cash discount is taken after quantity and trade discounts have been deducted. However, the cash discount always is taken before sales tax is added. This means the cash discount is subtracted from the amount due and then the sales tax is added.

REGULAR DATING

Regular dating indicates that the discount period begins with the date of the invoice. No consideration is given to when the goods arrived. When the last day of a cash discount period falls on a non-business day such as Sunday or a holiday, the discount is extended to the first day of business that follows. When working the problems in this chapter assume you do not have to contend with non-business days unless you are instructed otherwise. In examples or problems where the net due date is not given, assume it is 30 days.

An invoice with terms 3/10, 1/20, n/60 means that a 3% cash discount is granted if the bill is paid within 10 days of the invoice dating; a 1% cash discount is granted if the bill is paid within 20 days; and the net amount is due within 60 days. There is no cash discount granted if the bill is paid after 20 days. Simply, regular dating is defined as:

EQUATION 3.1

Regular Dating = Last Disc. Day is Date of Invoice + #Disc. Days Given

---

Problem On October 21, the Gingham Corner, a maternity shop, pays an invoice for baby carriers. The invoice was dated October 1 with terms 4/10, 2/20, n/30. What percent cash discount, if any, would the vendor allow?

Solution *Step 1* Find the last day a 4% cash discount will be allowed.

$$Last\ 4\%\ Disc.\ Day\ =\ Date\ of\ Invoice\ +\ \#Disc.\ Days$$

$$=\ October\ 1\ +\ 10$$

$$=\ October\ 11$$

Step 2 Find the last day a 2% cash discount will be allowed.

$$Last\ 2\%\ Disc.\ Day\ =\ Date\ of\ Invoice\ +\ \#Disc.\ Days$$

$$=\ October\ 1\ +\ 20$$

$$=\ October\ 21$$

Therefore, the Gingham Corner would qualify for a 2% cash discount.

Cash Discounts Given Regular Dating

The amount of cash discount is found by multiplying the discount percentage times the dollar amount of the invoice. The invoice cost should be adjusted already if quantity or trade discounts have been taken. Equation 3.2 illustrates the concept as follows:

EQUATION 3.2

$$\$Cash\ Discount\ =\ Discount\%\ (Invoice\ \$Cost)$$

Problem An invoice for an order from Colonial American Furniture costing $2,500 was dated April 17 and contained terms of 3/10, 1/20, n/60. If the bill was paid on May 6, what was the net amount due?

Solution *Step 1* Find the last day a 3% cash discount will be allowed.

$$Last\ 3\%\ Disc.\ Day\ =\ Date\ of\ Invoice\ +\ \#Disc.\ Days$$

$$=\ April\ 17\ +\ 10$$

$$=\ April\ 27$$

Step 2 Find the last day a 1% cash discount will be allowed.

$$Last\ 1\%\ Disc.\ Day\ =\ Date\ of\ Invoice\ +\ \#Disc.\ Days$$

$$=\ April\ 17\ +\ 20$$

$$=\ April\ 37\ -\ April\ 30\ =\ May\ 7$$

Because there are only 30 days in the month of April, we subtracted 30 to find the day of the next month.

Step 3 Find the value of the cash discount.

$$\$Cash\ Disc. = Disc.\%\ (Invoice\ \$Cost)$$

$$= 1\%\ (\$2,500.00)$$

$$= .01\ (\$2,500.00)$$

$$= \$25.00$$

Step 4 Find the net amount due.

$$Bal.\ Due = Invoice\ \$Cost - \$Cash\ Disc.$$

$$= \$2,500.00 - \$25.00$$

$$= \$2,475.00$$

Computer Drill 9: Cash Discounts

Cash Discounts is the name of the computer program that generates two types of problems for this section of the text. The types of problems available are:

- *Regular Dating*
- *Cash Discounts Given Regular Dating*

Assignments

1. An invoice dated May 14 accompanied a shipment of suits valued at $555. The manufacturer has granted the buyer terms of 3/10, n/60 and the buyer pays for the shipment on May 24. The net amount paid is $_____?

2. Coats were shipped to the retailer on April 19 at a cost of $2,265.00 The shipment is paid for on May 18 given terms of 3/10, n/30. The cash discount is $_____?

3. A buyer received a shipment of jackets with an invoice that totals $1,944.00, dated November 5. The Undercover Manufacturing Company has granted the buyer terms of 2/20, n/60 and the buyer's company pays for the shipment on November 14. The net amount paid is $_____?

4. A retailer received a shipment of shoes with an invoice that totals $2,274.00, dated November 28. The shipment is paid for on December 7 given terms of 2/10, n/30. The net amount paid is $_____?

5. An invoice dated March 7 accompanied a shipment of trousers valued at $3,353.00 with terms of 3/10, 1/20, n/60. The buyer's company pays for the shipment on March 17. The cash discount is $_____ ?

RECEIPT OF GOODS DATING

Retailers who are located great distances from a vendor or who are in areas where delivery may be delayed should request **receipt of goods dating (ROG)**. This means that the discount period begins when the goods arrive rather than the date on the invoice. If a delivery period is five days, there may not be time to check the merchandise when received or process the payment to meet a ten-day discount period.

Cash Discount Given ROG Dating

This form of dating may be written as 2/10, ROG or 2/10, n/30, ROG, both of which indicate a 2% discount is allowed for a 10-day period following the receipt of goods. Some companies may use the acronym AOG, which is synonymous with ROG and stands for arrival of goods. Again, this concept is demonstrated clearly in the following:

EQUATION 3.3

$$ROG \ = \ \textit{Last Disc. Day is the Day Goods Arrive} \ + \ \textit{#Disc. Days Given}$$

Problem   A shipment arrives on September 6 and the invoice is dated September 1. Terms are 3/10, n/60, ROG and the balance due is $540. What is the last day to pay for the shipment and still receive the discount? If the discount is taken, what is the amount due?

Solution   *Step 1* Find the last day for the cash discount.

$$\textit{Last Discount Day} = \textit{Day arrived} + 10$$

$$= \textit{September } 6 + 10$$

$$= \textit{September } 16$$

Step 2 Find the cash discount.

$$\$\textit{Cash Discount} = \textit{Discount\% (Invoice \$Cost)}$$

$$= 3\% \ (\$540.00)$$

$$= .03 \ (\$540.00)$$

$$= \$16.20$$

Step 3 Find the amount due.

$$\textit{Balance Due} = \textit{Invoice \$Cost} - \$\textit{Cash Discount}$$

$$= \$540.00 - \$16.20$$

$$= \$523.80$$

Computer Drill 10: Receipt of Goods Dating

If you would like to practice problems under this drill, select **Receipt of Goods Dating** from the drop down menu to the right of **Discounts, Terms, and Dating**. Since there is only one type of problem in this drill, selecting the capitalized RECEIPT OF GOODS DATING or the "Cash Discounts Given ROG Dating" option under the overall title will yield the same functionality within the program. Remember, you have the "solution" help button if you need it.

Assignments

1. Hats that cost $4,203.00 with terms 4/10 ROG were received by the Twin Company on November 6 with invoice dated November 5. If the buyer decided to pay the bill on November 17, then the net amount paid would be $_____ ?

2. Coats that cost $2,573.00 with terms 2/10 ROG were received by the Hope Company on January 30 with invoice dated January 21. If the buyer decided to pay the bill on February 8, then the net amount paid would be $_____ ?

3. Coolers that cost $2,038.00 with terms 3/10 ROG were recieved by the Hendel Company on August 26 with an invoice dated August 23. If the buyer decided to pay the bill on September 5, then the cash discount would be $_____ ?

4. Books that cost $3,857.00 with terms 3/10 ROG were received by the Bookworm Company on December 25 with an invoice dated December 22. If the buyer decided to pay the bill on January 4, then the cash discount would be $_____ ?

END OF MONTH DATING

In many instances a dating may include the acronym EOM. This is an abbreviation for **end of month dating (EOM)**. This term indicates that the number of days allowed for the cash discount begins after the end of the month. Therefore, a dating such as 4/10, EOM, n/60 means that a 4% cash discount is allowed if the bill is paid within the first 10 days of the following month. The net amount is due 60 days after the first day of the discount period.

Cash Discount Given EOM Dating Before 25th

If a purchase is billed with terms of 2/10, EOM, n/60, the payment must be made ten days after the end of the month the invoice was issued to receive a 2% discount. The net amount is due 60 days from the day the discount period begins. This is shown clearly in the following:

EQUATION 3.4

$$EOM = \textit{If Invoice is Dated Before 25th, the Last Disc. Day is the EOM + #Disc. Days}$$

Problem An invoice dated August 12 arrives August 27 with a balance due of $425. Terms of the bill are 2/10, EOM, n/30. What is the last day to earn the cash discount? What is the net amount due if the bill was paid on September 8?

Solution *Step 1* Find the last day for the discount.

$$Last\ Discount\ Day = End\ of\ Month + 10\ days$$

$$= August\ 31 + 10$$

$$= September\ 10$$

Step 2 Find cash discount if any. Because the bill was paid before September 10, a 2% cash discount is allowed.

$$\$Cash\ Discount = Discount\%\ (Invoice\ \$Cost)$$

$$= 2\%\ (\$425.00)$$

$$= .02\ (\$425.00)$$

$$= \$8.50$$

Step 3 Find net amount due.

$$Balance\ Due = Invoice\ \$Cost - \$Cash\ Discount$$

$$= \$425.00 - \$8.50$$

$$= \$416.50$$

Cash Discount Given EOM Dating On or After 25th

Generally, invoices that are dated on or after the 25th of the month with an EOM dating are considered to be purchased in the following month. This means that an invoice dating of March 26 and terms of 5/10, EOM would not have to be paid until May 10 to receive the 5% discount. This principle is stated simply in the following:

EQUATION 3.5

EOM = If Invoice is Dated On or After 25th, Last Disc. Day is End of Next Month + #Disc. Days Specified

---

Problem   The Egghead Bookstore received a shipment of books on August 29. The invoice dated August 27 read "Balance due $365" with terms "3/10, EOM, n/60". What was the last date for the discount? What was the balance due on that date?

Solution   *Step 1* Find the last day to earn the discount.

$$Last\ Discount\ Day = End\ of\ Next\ Month + 10\ days$$

$$= September\ 30 + 10\ days$$

$$= October\ 10$$

Step 2 Find the cash discount.

$$\$Cash\ Discount = Discount\%\ (Invoice\ \$Cost)$$

$$= 3\%\ (\$365.00)$$

$$= .03\ (\$365.00)$$

$$= \$10.95$$

Step 3 Find the balance due.

$$Balance\ Due = Invoice\ \$Cost - \$Cash\ Discount$$

$$= \$365.00 - \$10.95$$

$$= \$354.05$$

Computer Drill 11: End of Month Dating

End of Month Dating is the name of the computer program that generates two types of problems for this section of the text. The types of problems available are:

- *Cash Discount Given EOM dating before 25th*
- *Cash Discount Given EOM dating after 25th*

Assignments

1. The Fort Fun Company received a statement with terms of 3/10, EOM, n/60. The invoice amount was $555.00 and was dated May 14. To receive the discount, the invoice must be paid by _____?

2. As a buyer for the Ouji Company, you receive an invoice with terms 4/10, EOM, n/90. The invoice amount was $2,265.00 and was dated April 19. To receive the discount, the invoice must be paid by _____?

3. The Hiss Company purchased goods with negotiated terms of 5/10, EOM, n/60. The invoice amount was $4,203.00 and was dated November 5. If the invoice is paid by December 10, the amount owed will be $_____?

4. As a buyer for the Ristray Company, you receive an invoice with terms 2/10, EOM, n/60. The invoice amount was $2,038.00 and was dated August 23. The last day to pay the invoice without incurring a finance charge is _____?

5. The Culpron Corporation purchased goods with negotiated terms of 3/10, EOM, n/90. The invoice amount was $2,274.00 and was dated November 28. To receive the discount, the invoice must be paid by _____?

EXTRA DATING

Extra dating is a form of dating that extends the number of days allowed for a discount. The most common reason for granting such terms is to encourage early buying. While an order that is placed before the height of the normal buying period stimulates the manufacturer's business, the retailer will not receive income from sales until the season arrives. Consequently, extra dating allows the manufacturer to receive early orders, which in turn clear the storage area and allow room for new goods. The retailer is assured of having goods and is not obligated to pay immediately.

Cash Discount Given Extra Dating

An X or the word extra signifies that the period during which a cash discount is available is extended. Thus the terms 3/10, 60X, n/90 or 3/10, 60 extra, net 90 indicate that a 3% discount is allowed if the bill is paid within 70 days (10 + 60) from the date of the invoice. In any case, the net amount must be paid in 90 days. Extra dating is defined again as follows:

EQUATION 3.6

Extra Dating = Last Disc. Day is Date of Invoice + # Disc. Days + Extra Days

Problem To avoid the Christmas rush, the housewares buyer placed an order for electric mixers amounting to $850. The invoice dated September 26 with terms of 4/10, 60X, n/90 was paid on December 3. How much did the store have to pay?

Solution *Step 1* Find the last day to pay and receive the discount.

Last Disc. Day = Date of Invoice + #Disc. Days + Extra Days

$= September\ 26\ +\ 10\ days\ +\ 60\ days$

$= September\ 26\ +\ 70\ days$

$= 4\ in\ Sept.\ +\ 31\ in\ Oct.\ +\ 30\ in\ Nov.\ +\ 5\ in\ Dec.$

$= December\ 5$

Step 2 Find the cash discount.

$Cash\ Disc. = Disc.\%\ (Invoice\ \$Cost)$

$= 4\%\ (\$850.00)$

$= .04\ (\$850.00)$

$= \$34.00$

Step 3 Find the balance due.

$$Balance\ Due = Invoice\ \$Cost - \$Cash\ Disc.$$

$$= \$850.00 - \$34.00$$

$$= \$816.00$$

Computer Drill 12: Extra Dating

If you would like to practice problems under this drill, select **Extra Dating** from the drop down menu to the right of **Discounts, Terms, and Dating**. Since there is only one type of problem in this drill, selecting the capitalized EXTRA DATING or the "Cash Discounts Given Extra Dating" option under the overall title will yield the same functionality within the program. Remember, you have the "solution" help button if you need it.

Assignments

1. Hats that cost $3,353.00 with terms 3/10, 30X, n/60 were received by the Maxy Company on April 16. If the invoice was dated March 7 and the buyer decided to pay the bill on April 17, the net amount paid would be $_____?

[handwritten notes: $3252.41; Mar 7 +10 / Mar17 +30 / Apr 17]

[handwritten notes: $3,353.00   3/10 - 30X   n/60   Mar 7 - 3%   Mar 17 / 30 + / Apr 17   Apr 8]

2. Tool boxes that cost $2,038.00 with terms 1/10, 60X, n/90 were received by the Remo Corporation on August 26. If the invoice was dated August 23 and the buyer decided to pay the bill on October 31, the cash discount would be $_____?

3. Stuffed toys that cost $1,891.00 with terms 2/10, 60X, n/120 were received by the Great American Bear Company on December 6 with an invoice dated November 28. If the buyer decided to pay the bill on March 8, the net amount paid would be $_____?

4. Tableware that cost $3,857.00 with terms 2/10, 60X, n/90 were received by the Tabletop Company on December 25 with an invoice dated December 22. If the buyer decided to pay the bill on March 2, the cash discount would be $_____?

ANTICIPATION

Anticipation is an additional discount that is granted when a bill is paid before it is due. Anticipation serves as an incentive to pay bills early, thus allowing the vendor use of the store's money. Most vendors allow anticipation only if the bill is paid before the cash discount period expires. Anticipation normally is calculated from the cost recorded on the invoice ignoring cash discounts. The two discounts are subtracted simultaneously. Stores that pay their bill early can receive a discount based on the current rate of interest and the amount of extra time the manufacturer has the retailer's money. When money is tight the interest rate is high and when the rate becomes too high, many vendors refuse to grant anticipation. The granting of anticipation should be part of the purchasing agreement that has been negotiated between the buyer and the vendor and should never be assumed. Additionally, conditions for anticipation vary, such as some vendors require the store to take the cash discount first and then base anticipation on the reduced cost. This is not to buyer's advantage because it results in a higher cost figure. This type of condition needs to be negotiated by the buyer and vendor also.

Dollar Anticipation

Anticipation is a dollar discount based on a percentage of the invoice cost. Because interest rates usually are given as a yearly percentage, we have to convert this figure to a daily basis and multiply by the number of days worth of anticipation. In these calculations, the number of days in a year is taken as 360. Thus, anticipation is the product of the yearly interest rate, the invoice cost, and the number of days anticipated divided by 360 days. The formula for calculating dollar anticipation is as follows:

EQUATION 3.7

$$\$Anticipation = (\%\,Yearly\,Interest)\,(Invoice\,\$Cost)\left(\frac{\#Days\,Anticipated}{360}\right)$$

Problem

A bill for \$2,000 with terms of 3/10, 90 extra is paid in 40 days. The yearly interest rate is $6\frac{1}{2}\%$. What is the anticipation?

Solution   *Step 1* Find the number of days anticipated.

$$\#Days\,Anticipated = \#Days\,for\,Discount - \#Days\,Until\,Paid$$

$$= (10 + 90) - 40$$

$$= 100 - 40$$

$$= 60$$

Step 2 Find the anticipation.

$$\$Anticipation = (\%\,Yearly\ Int.)\ (Invoice\ \$Cost)\left(\frac{\#Days\ Anticipated}{360}\right)$$

$$= 6.5\%\ (\$2,000.00)\left(\frac{60}{360}\right)$$

$$= .065\ (\$2,000.00)\ .1667$$

$$= \$21.67$$

Balance Due Given Anticipation and Cash Discounts

As stated earlier, the cash discount is calculated as a percentage of the cost recorded on the invoice. Anticipation is an additional discount that is calculated as a percentage of this same cost figure. The two discounts then are subtracted from the cost to give the net amount of the invoice. This net amount is the balance due. (Please note that for the purposes of illustration we are ignoring such possibilities as transportation charges and taxes.) The formula for calculating the balance due given anticipation and cash discounts is stated clearly in the following:

EQUATION 3.8

$$Balance\ Due\ =\ Invoice\ \$Cost\ -\ \$Cash\ Discount\ -\ \$Anticipation$$

Problem   Doll houses that have a quoted cost of $500 were delivered to the toy department on November 21 with terms of 3/10 ROG, 30X plus anticipation. Using an 8% yearly interest rate, how much would the store remit if the bill was paid on December 1?

Solution   *Step 1* Find the number of days anticipated.

$$\#Days\ Anticipated = \#Days\ for\ Discount\ -\ \#Days\ Until\ Paid$$

$$= 10 + 30 - 10$$

$$= 30$$

Step 2 Find the anticipation.

$$\$Anticipation = (\%\,Yearly\ Int.)\ (Inv.\ \$Cost)\left(\frac{\#Days\ Ant'd.}{360}\right)$$

$$= 8\%\ (\$500.00)\left(\frac{30}{360}\right)$$

$$= .08\ (\$500.00)\ (.0833)$$

$$= \$3.33$$

Step 3 Find the cash discount.

$$Last\ Disc.\ Day = Day\ Arrived\ +\ \#Disc.\ Days\ Given$$

$$= November\ 21\ +\ 10$$

$$= December\ 1$$

Step 4 Find the amount due.

$$\$Cash\ Disc. = (Disc.\%)\ Invoice\ \$Cost$$

$$= (3\%)\ \$500.00$$

$$= (.03)\ \$500.0$$

$$= \$15.00$$

Step 5 Find the amount due.

$$Bal.\ Due = Inv.\ \$Cost\ -\ \$Cash\ Disc.\ -\ \$Anticipation$$

$$= \$500.00\ -\ \$15.00\ -\ \$3.33$$

$$= \$481.67$$

Computer Drill 13: Anticipation

Anticipation is the name of the computer program that generates two types of problems for this section of the text. The types of problems available are:

- *Dollar Anticipation*
- *Balance Due Given Anticipation and Cash Discounts*

Assignments

1. A bill dated January 21 for the amount of $360.00 is received by the Star Company with terms of 3/30X. If the balance is paid in 35 days, how much would the buyer pay if the anticipation granted is 8.25%?

2. The buyer for Island Silk has negotiated for terms of 5/60X, plus 8.50% anticipation on an invoice of $1,080.00. What is the maximum anticipation that can be obtained?

3. The Lily Company has been granted a 8.50% anticipation for a statement dated February 23 (6/90X). The invoice for $6,400.00 is paid April 9. The company will pay $_____.

4. A 10.00% anticipation has been granted to the Opal Company for a statement dated December 11 (5/30 extra). The invoice for $5,400.00 is paid January 8. By paying the invoice at this time, the company will save $_____.

5. An invoice from the Menx Company with terms 6/60 extra is paid 36 days after the date of billing. What is the payment if anticipation is 7.75% and the invoice amount is $2,520.00?

<table>
<tr><td colspan="2" align="center">**FIGURE 3.1**</td><td colspan="2" align="center">**FIGURE 3.2**</td></tr>
<tr><td>*Quantity*</td><td>*%Discount*</td><td>*$Amount*</td><td>*%Discount*</td></tr>
<tr><td>1-5 dozen</td><td>0%</td><td>under $200</td><td>0%</td></tr>
<tr><td>6-12 dozen</td><td>1%</td><td>$200 to $499</td><td>1%</td></tr>
<tr><td>13-25 dozen</td><td>2%</td><td>$500 to $1,000</td><td>3%</td></tr>
<tr><td>over 25 dozen</td><td>3%</td><td>more than $1,000</td><td>5%</td></tr>
</table>

QUANTITY DISCOUNTS

A **quantity discount** is granted based on the number of items purchased. This discount is intended to encourage larger volume purchases. The most obvious reason for encouraging larger purchases is to increase the sales volume. The manufacturer or distributor also can benefit through the lowering of selling costs because large orders mean less paper work, less sales time, and lower shipping costs per item. Large orders also may help cut costs when the manufacturer is purchasing raw materials and producing the goods.

Many retailers earn quantity discounts by placing blanket orders. Blanket orders are placed for a large quantity of staple items that should always be in stock. These items are to be billed and shipped as they are required by the retailer. Essentially, the items are not stored at the retailer's expense. However, the manufacturer or distributor benefits from lower selling and production costs.

To protect the smaller retailer who cannot afford large orders, the manufacturer must comply with federal legislation regulating discounts, which simply states that the size of the discount given to the retailer cannot exceed the savings accrued by the manufacturer.

Noncumulative Quantity Discounts

The **noncumulative quantity discount** indicates that the discount is based on one order for goods purchased at a single time and delivered to one destination. If the order is above a certain minimum purchase, a discount is granted. In some instances, a discount schedule indicates the discount rate for each size of purchase, as shown in Figure 3.1. In other cases, the discount schedule refers to the value of the purchase, as presented in Figure 3.2.

The formula is essentially the same as for most discounts. The dollar discount value equals the noncumulative quantity discount percentage times the cost, illustrated simply in the following:

EQUATION 3.9

$$\textit{Noncumulative Quan. \$Disc.} = \left(\frac{\textit{Noncumulative Quan. Disc.\%}}{100\%} \right) \textit{\$Cost}$$

Problem   A buyer for Henson's Men's Wear placed an order for golf shirts amounting to $635. The vendor grants noncumulative quantity discounts in the following manner:

$Amount	Discount
$300 − $449	1%
$450 − $750	2.5%
over $750	3%

What is the invoice charge for the shirts?

Solution   *Step 1* Find the dollar discount.

$$Noncumulative\ Quan.\ \$Disc. = \left(\frac{Noncumulative\ Quan.\ Disc.\%}{100\%}\right)\$Cost$$

$$= \left(\frac{2.5\%}{100\%}\right)\$635.00$$

$$= .025\ (\$635.00)$$

$$= \$15.88$$

Step 2 Find the invoice charge.

$$Balance\ Due = \$Cost - \$Discount$$

$$= \$635.00 - \$15.88$$

$$= \$619.12$$

Problem   A vendor for household linens used the rates given in Figure 3.1 to grant quantity discounts. You have just ordered seven dozen towels in assorted colors for $185. How much do you expect the invoice to be?

Solution   *Step 1* Find the dollar discount.

$$Noncumulative\ \$Disc. = \left(\frac{Noncumulative\ Quan.\ Disc.\%}{100\%}\right)\$Cost$$

$$= \left(\frac{1\%}{100\%}\right)\$185.00$$

$$= (.01)\ \$185.00$$

$$= \$1.85$$

Step 2 Find the net amount.

$$Balance\ Due = \$Cost - \$Discount$$

$$= \$185.00 - \$1.85$$

$$= \$183.15$$

FIGURE 3.3

Total Purchases For Season	%Discount
less than $400	0%
$400 - $1,499	2%
$1,500 - $3,999	4%
$4,000 - $10,000	6%
over $10,000	8%

FIGURE 3.4

Total Quantity	%Discount
less 12 dozen	0%
12 - 20 dozen	2%
21 - 40 dozen	4%
over 40 dozen	5%

Cumulative Quantity Discounts

A **cumulative quantity discount** is granted for the total amount purchased over a given period of time. The effect of several purchases is then cumulative. Additionally, deliveries may be made to several different locations. Total purchases for a season from a specific company would be compared to the discount schedule and then the discount would be granted. Again, the discount schedule might be in dollars or it may be in numbers of items, as demonstrated in Figure 3.3 and Figure 3.4.

The cumulative discount, because of its method of calculation sometimes is referred to as a deferred discount. The equation is similar to that for noncumulative quantity discounts, as is shown in the following formula:

EQUATION 3.10

$$Cumulative\ \$Discount = \left(\frac{Cumulative\ Discount\ \%}{100\%}\right)\$Cost$$

Problem The manufacturer's records show that the Eames Company ordered $1,000 worth of merchandise in March, $3,000 in April, $8,000 in May and $1,000 in June. If the manufacturer used Figure 3.3 as the discount schedule, how much was the discount granted to the Eames Company?

Solution *Step 1* Total the amount of purchase.

$$\$Cost = \$March + \$April + \$May + \$June$$

$$= \$1,000.00 + \$3,000.00 + \$8,000.00 + \$1,000.00$$

$$= \$13,000.00$$

Step 2 Find discount value using Figure 3.3.

$$Cumulative\ \$Discount = \left(\frac{Cumulative\ Discount\%}{100\%}\right)\$Cost$$

$$= \left(\frac{8\%}{100\%}\right)\$13,000.00$$

$$= (.08)\ \$13,000.00$$

$$= \$1,040.00$$

Problem During the season, Breezy's, a resort shop, purchased eight dozen bikinis, six dozen swim suits, and ten dozen coverups. The total purchases amounted to $2,250. Using Figure 3.4, find the net cost of the total order.

Solution *Step 1* Find the total number of items purchased.

$$Total \; \#Dozen = 8 \; Dozen + 6 \; Dozen + 10 \; Dozen$$

$$= 24 \; Dozen$$

Step 2 Find the dollar discount.

$$Cumulative \; \$Discount = \left(\frac{Cumulative \; Discount\%}{100\%} \right) \$Cost$$

$$= \left(\frac{4\%}{100\%} \right) \$2,250.00$$

$$= (.04) \; \$2,250.00$$

$$= \$90.00$$

Step 3 Find the net amount.

$$Balance \; Due = \$Cost - \$Discount$$

$$= \$2,250.00 - \$90.00$$

$$= \$2,160.00$$

Computer Drill 14: Quantity Discounts

Quantity Discounts is the name of the computer program that generates two types of problems for this section of the text. The types of problems available are:

- *Noncumulative Quantity Discounts*
- *Cumulative Quantity Discounts*

Assignments

1. The vendor granted the following quantity discounts if the buyer purchased in lots of:

1 to 5 dozen	(0.0 %)
6 to 10 dozen	(1.00 %)
11 to 15 dozen	(2.00 %)
Over 15 dozen	(3.00 %)

The buyer purchased four dozen robes at $117.00 per dozen. If this were the only discount granted for this purchase, the invoice payment would be $_____ .

2. The vendor granted the following discounts if the buyer purchased in lots of:

1 to 10 dozen	(0.0 %)
11 to 25 dozen	(1.00 %)
26 to 50 dozen	(2.00 %)
Over 50 dozen	(3.00 %)

A buyer purchased 67 dozen toys at $11.00 per dozen. If this were the only discount granted for this purchase, the invoice payment would be $_____ .

3. The vendor granted the following discounts if the buyer purchased in dollar amounts of:

Less than $200.00	(0.0 %)
$200.00 to $500.00	(1.00 %)
$501.00 to $1,000.00	(1.50 %)
More than $1,000.00	(2.00 %)

A buyer purchased $861.00 worth of belt buckles. The quantity discount for this purchase would be _____ .

TRADE DISCOUNTS

Trade discounts are a reduction in the manufacturers' quoted catalogue price as a means of establishing cost. These discounts are granted to people who provide various services in the total distribution process of a product. The Robinson-Patman Act of 1936 indicates that prices must be in keeping with the marketing functions performed. These functions might include such services as providing delivery or storage, creating promotional plans and properties, or extending credit. The more marketing responsibilities one has, therefore, the greater the justification for a larger trade discount. A trade discount can be taken without considering when the bill was paid. Goods may be sold directly to the retailer or there may be one or two middlemen who handle the goods passing from the manufacturer to the retailer.

Trade discounts are expressed as a single percentage or a series of percentages deducted from the list price, or recommended retail price. A buyer who performs most of the functions in the distribution chain may receive all of the percentage discounts, while one who works through two different middlemen and performs very few functions may receive only one discount. Companies that have printed catalogues find this method of pricing simpler than reprinting a catalogue with new list prices. They are able to reflect a change in the cost of manufacturing their product by changing the trade discount percentages.

Dollar Trade Discounts

A manufacturer or wholesaler publishes a catalogue or listing of the suggested selling price of goods they produce or sell. These are referred to as "list prices" or "suggested retail prices". The difference between the list price and the invoice cost for the merchandise is the trade discount. When you receive your invoice or bill, the discounts should be taken already.

EQUATION 3.11

$$Trade\ \$Discount\ =\ List\ Price\ -\ Invoice\ \$Cost$$

Problem   The list price of an electronic calculator is \$58.95 and the retailer purchases them for \$31 each. What is the dollar value of the retailer's trade discount?

Solution

$$Trade\ \$Discount\ =\ List\ Price\ -\ Invoice\ \$Cost$$
$$=\ \$58.95\ -\ \$31.00$$
$$=\ \$27.95$$

Trade Discount Percentage

For the retailer, the trade dollar discount is a percentage of the list price. The use of a percent discount simplifies the manufacturer's or vendor's printed matter in that each discounted price does not have to be stated. A trade discount percentage is multiplied by the list price to obtain the trade dollar discount, as shown in the following:

EQUATION 3.12

$$\textit{Trade \$Discount} = \left(\frac{\textit{Trade Discount\%}}{100\%} \right) \textit{List Price}$$

Problem   Men's hip boots have a suggested retail price of $25. The buyer for Buck Speers purchases them for $16.25 each. What was the buyer's trade discount percentage?

Solution   *Step 1* Find the dollar value of the trade discount.

$$\textit{Trade \$Discount} = \textit{List Price} - \textit{Invoice \$Cost}$$

$$= \$25.00 - \$16.25$$

$$= \$8.75$$

Step 2 Rewrite equation 3.12 to calculate the trade discount percentage.

$$\textit{Trade Discount\%} = \left(\frac{\textit{Trade \$Discount}}{\textit{List Price}} \right) 100\%$$

$$= \left(\frac{\$8.75}{\$25.00} \right) 100\%$$

$$= (.35)\, 100\%$$

$$= 35\%$$

Net Price Given Trade Discount Percentage

The net price (i.e., the cost of the item to the retailer), is the difference between the list price and the dollar value of the trade discounts. In this discussion of net price we are assuming no other discounts are involved. First, we invert *equation 3.11* for solving the dollar invoice cost:

$$\textit{Invoice \$Cost} = \textit{List Price} - \textit{Trade \$Discount}$$

Then, substitute the basic formula for the trade discount percent for the trade dollar discount:

$$\textit{Invoice \$Cost} = \textit{List Price} - \left(\frac{\textit{Trade Discount\%}}{100\%} \right) \textit{List Price}$$

Next, factor out the list price, using the complement of the trade discount percent, because you are calculating the dollar cost:

$$\textit{Invoice \$Cost} = \textit{List Price} \left(\frac{100\% - \textit{Trade Discount\%}}{100\%} \right)$$

Consequently, the net price is the product of the list price and the complement of the trade discount percentage divided by 100%, as illustrated in the following:

EQUATION 3.13

$$Invoice\ \$Cost\ =\ List\ Price\left(\frac{Complement\ of\ Trade\ Discount\%}{100\%}\right)$$

Problem The buyer for the Pillar Department Store orders a bookcase listed at $169 less 40%. This means that the buyer's trade discount is 40%. How much did the bookcase cost the buyer?

Solution $Invoice\ \$Cost\ =\ List\ Price\left(\dfrac{Complement\ of\ Trade\ Discount\%}{100\%}\right)$

$$=\ \$169.00\left(\frac{100\%\ -\ 40\%}{100\%}\right)$$

$$=\ \$169.00\left(\frac{60\%}{100\%}\right)$$

$$=\ \$169.00\ (.60)$$

$$=\ \$101.40$$

Multiple Trade Discounts

A manufacturer may indicate more than one trade discount depending on the number of functions to be performed. This is called a **multiple trade discount**. The manufacturer may use middlemen or the retailer may perform the functions and obtain these discounts. Chain or multiple discounts may be written as 30, 20, 10 or they may be written less 30, less 20, less 10. This means that the retailer is granted 30% off the list price, the second wholesaler receives 20% off the retailer's cost and the first wholesaler receives 10% off the second wholesaler's cost. These discounts are NOT additive. In other words, you do not add the three discounts together and get a 60% discount. You must go through the series of discounts as shown in Figure 3.5:

FIGURE 3.5

1st discount	2nd discount	3rd discount	
Retailer/Buyer —>	Second Wholesaler —>	First Wholesaler —>	Manufacturer
list price	retailer/buyer price	2nd wholesaler price	net cost
minus 30%	minus 20%	minus 10%	

To find the manufacturer's net price we have to take the discounts one at a time and find the cost to the retailer and each middleman. This is equivalent to determining the cost by taking the product of the list price and the complement of each discount of interest. The product of the complement sometimes is called the on percentage. The formula for this calculation is as follows:

EQUATION 3.14

$$Invoice\ \$Cost\ =\ List\ Price \left(\frac{Complement\ 1st\ Disc.\% \times Complement\ nth\ Disc.\%}{100\%} \right)$$

Problem   The manufacturer's catalogue lists an electric typewriter for $290 less 40, less 25, less 10. What is the cost to the first wholesaler?

Solution

$$Invoice\ \$Cost\ =$$

$$List\ Price \left(\frac{Comp.\ 1st\ Disc.\% \times Comp.\ 2nd\ Disc.\% \times Comp.\ 3rd\ Disc.\%}{100\%} \right)$$

Step 1 Find the cost to the retailer/buyer.

$$= \$290.00 \left(\frac{100\% - 40\%}{100\%} \right)$$

$$= \$290.00\ (.60)$$

$$= \$174.00$$

Step 2 Find the cost to the second wholesaler.

$$= \$174.00 \left(\frac{100\% - 25\%}{100\%} \right)$$

$$= \$174.00\ (.75)$$

$$= \$130.50$$

Step 3 Find the cost to the first wholesaler.

$$= \$130.50 \left(\frac{100\% - 10\%}{100\%} \right)$$

$$= \$130.50\ (.90)$$

$$= \$117.45$$

Problem The list price for corner cabinets is $180/30, 20, 10. What is the dollar value of the trade discount granted to the second wholesaler?

Solution *Step 1* Find the cost to the second wholesaler.

$$Inv.\ \$Cost = List\ Price\ (Comp.\ 1st\ Disc.\%)(Comp.\ 2nd\ Disc.\%)$$

$$= \$180.00\left(\frac{100\% - 30\%}{100\%}\right)\left(\frac{100\% - 20\%}{100\%}\right)$$

$$= \$180.00\ (.70)(.80)$$

$$= \$100.80$$

Step 2 Find the dollar value of the trade discount.

$$Trade\ \$Discount = List\ Price - Invoice\ \$Cost$$

$$= \$180.00 - \$100.80$$

$$= \$79.20$$

Computer Drill 15: Trade Discounts

Trade Discounts is the name of the computer program that generates four types of problems for this section of the text. The types of problems available are:

- *Dollar Trade Discounts*
- *Trade Discount Percentage*
- *Net Price Given Trade Discount Percentage*
- *Multiple Trade Discounts*

Assignments

1. The Opal Manufacturing Company lists shirts at $117.00 per box. The manufacturer sells through wholesalers for distribution to retailers and trade discounts of 20/10 were offered to the buyer. How much should this middleman pay for the merchandise?

2. The buyer from Timelines acquires watches from a manufacturer with a list price of $86.00 per carton. Trade discounts of less 30, less 10, less 5 were offered to the buyer. Providing there were no other discounts, how much did the buyer pay for the merchandise?

3. Boots are purchased from the Harding Manufacturing Company at $227.00 per item. Wholesalers are utilized in the distribution process and trade discounts of 30, 20, 10 were offered to the buyer. How much would the second wholesaler pay for the merchandise?

4. The Kelly Manufacturer's list price for jeans was $113.00 per dozen. Trade discounts of less 20, less 15, less 5 were offered to the buyer. Find the net price of the jeans if no other discounts were allowed.

LOADING THE INVOICE

Cash discounts are very important to store profits. The practice of **loading the invoice** increases both the cost and the cash discounts. The invoice will look like the retailer paid more for the merchandise but also received a higher discount percentage. The vendor receives the same amount of money either way with or without loading. Some buyers try to impress their managers with their negotiating prowess by asking the vendor to load the invoice and sometimes management will encourage the practice to establish a standard discount percentage. However, when cash discounts are considered as additional income, the markups are based on the invoice cost and either the customer ends up paying more for the goods or the markdown increases. We mention this practice only to let you know it exists.

Computer Drill 16: All Discounts

To practice all type of discount problems, highlight and select "Chapter Three" from the drop down menu to the right of **Discounts, Terms, and Dating**. The purpose of this section is to integrate the various forms of discounts you have learned to calculate. The order of these problems will be random, so this section will provide an excellent opportunity for you to test your mastery of discounts, terms, and dating. Thus, if you decide you need an additional drill on a specific problem type you should stop this program and choose the name of the program that will generate the specific problem type you desire. For your convenience the program names are repeated here:

- *Cash Discounts*
- *Receipt of Goods Dating*
- *End of Month Dating*
- *Extra Dating*
- *Anticipation*
- *Quantity Discounts*
- *Trade Discounts*

Assignments

1. Evening dresses that cost $2,573.00 with terms 4/10, 30X, n/60 were received by the Bela Company on January 30 with an invoice dated January 21. If the buyer decided to pay the bill on March 4, then the net amount paid would be $_____?

2. A bill dated February 9 for the amount of $360.00 is received by the Eckman Company with terms 6/90X. If the balance is paid in 30 days, how much would the buyer pay if the anticipation granted is 7.50%?

3. The vendor granted the following discounts if the buyer purchased in dollar amounts of:

Less than $100.00	(0.0 %)
$100.00 to $250.00	(1.00 %)
$251.00 to $500.00	(1.50 %)
More than $500.00	(2.00 %)

A buyer purchased $310.00 worth of belts. If this was the only discount granted for this purchase, the invoice payment would be $_____?

4. Jackets that cost $4,255.00 with terms 4/10 ROG were received by the Closet Case on December 6 with an invoice dated November 28. If the buyer decided to pay the bill on December 17, then the net amount paid would be _____?

5. The Kara Company received a statement with terms of 6/10, EOM, n/60. The invoice amount was $3,507.00 and was dated January 26. The last day to pay the invoice without incurring a finance charge was _____?

6. The buyer for men's furnishings acquires hosiery from a manufacturer with a list price of $57.00 per item. Trade discounts of 30/20/10 were offered to the buyer. Providing there were no other discounts, how much did the buyer pay for the item?

7. The Corbet Company buyer has negotiated terms of 3/30X plus 8.75% anticipation on an invoice of $2,880.00. What is the maximum anticipation that can be obtained?

8. An invoice dated January 21 accompanied a shipment of musical instruments valued at $3,507.00. The shipment is paid on February 10 given terms of 3/10, n/30. The cash discount is $_____?

9. Beachwear that cost $4,203.00 with terms 3/10, 90X, n/120 was received by the Hilo Company on November 6, with an invoice dated November 5. If the buyer decided to pay the bill on February 14, then the net amount paid would be _____?

10. Intimate apparel was shipped to the retailer on November 10 at a cost of $735.00 with terms of 2/10, 1/20, n/30. On November 30, the balance due on the shipment is mailed. The cash discount is $_____?

11. The Loveline Manufacturing Company lists lipstick at $17.00 per box. The manufacturer sells through wholesalers for distribution to retailers and trade discounts of 30/10/5 were offered to the buyer. How much would the retailer pay for the merchandise?

12. A vendor granted the following discounts if the buyer purchased toys in lots of:

1 to 10 dozen	(0.0 %)
11 to 25 dozen	(1.00 %)
26 to 50 dozen	(1.50 %)
Over 50 dozen	(2.00 %)

A buyer purchased 36 dozen toys at $16.00 per dozen. If this was the only discount granted for this purchase, the invoice payment would be _____?

13. The Ouji Company received a statement with terms of 4/10, EOM, n/90. The invoice amount was $3,353.00 and was dated March 26. The last day to pay the invoice without incurring a financial charge was _____?

14. The manufacturer's list price for bookcases was $350.00 per dozen. Trade discounts of 25, 10 were offered to the buyer. Providing there were no other discounts, how much did the buyer pay for the merchandise?

15. A tabletop buyer received a shipment of baskets with an invoice totaling $868.00. It was dated February 23 with terms of 2/10, 1/20, n/60. The buyer decides to pay for the shipment on March 4. The cash discount is $_____?

CHAPTER FOUR

Assessing Stock Activity

In this chapter we will discuss some of the various methods used in the assessment of inventory or stock. The words **stock** and **inventory** are used interchangeably in this text to represent the merchandise that is to be sold to the ultimate consumer. Stock control and assessment are essential to a buyer's or store owner's success because inventory represents the primary investment aside from the physical operating space. Ideally the retailer wants a balanced inventory. This means that the amount of inventory in the store balances with the anticipated sales volume. However, there are four very typical unbalanced conditions that can occur. These conditions are:

1. **Out-of-stock**. Being out-of-stock means that the retailer no longer has a product in stock. When a customer enters the store to purchase a product and the options or products available to the customer are not there or are too limited to offer a good selection, the retailer will lose out on potential sales. Because the product is not available and a purchase is not made, the retailer will experience a loss of sales due to these low inventory levels. Consequently, the low inventory that results in low sales volume then will impact the profit margin. If potential customers continue to come to the retailer and are not able to find the products or services they desire, that retailer likely will experience a loss of traffic and customer loyalty. Consumers then will seek out new or different retailers to serve their needs and wants.

2. **Overstocked**. An overstocked position occurs when the retailer carries more inventory than is necessary to meet customer's needs and wants. When inventories are excessively high the retailer has invested more money in buying merchandise than is necessary, which is an inefficient use of capital. When inventory levels are high the retailer will experience lower profits due to unnecessary storage costs for the merchandise that is not on the sales floor. There also will be high markdown risks due to this overstocked merchandise that is not sold.

3. **Shortages**. Shortages occur when merchandise is missing, miscounted, or not recorded properly. When the dollar value of a physical count of merchandise in the store is less than the inventory shown in the retailer's inventory records, there is a **stock shortage**. The most frequent reason for

shortage is theft; most often pilferage by employees. However, shortages also can occur due to human error in counting merchandise, when items are misplaced and fail to be counted, or because merchandise transferred from one store to another is not recorded correctly. Therefore, all shortages — no matter what the cause — are treated as a form of reduction and must be considered when planning inventory.

4. **Excessive markdowns**. If merchandise does not sell at its current price, the retailer will begin marking down the price to make it more attractive to the consumer. Some product areas, such as fashion apparel, tend to have extremely large overall markdown percentages of up to twenty percent. When large markdowns are considered normal for a business, the retailer must build an inventory plan that takes these reductions into account. If high markdowns are not considered, the inventory available will fall short of the amount needed to cover anticipated sales.

This chapter will expose you to tools that can aid in balancing your inventory. This is done by three mathematical aids called shortage, turnover, and the stock-to-sales ratio. The shortage figure will tell a retailer if all items of stock are accounted for or if any items are missing. The turnover figure will tell the retailer how rapidly the stock is selling, and the stock-to-sales ratio will reflect the amount of stock that is available to meet sales demand. Turnover figures and stock-sales ratios are both used as measures of efficiency in a store or department and can be used for comparison purposes.

STOCK SHORTAGE

Shortages occur for various reasons. There may be errors in recording transfers, errors in counting merchandise, or even errors in such customer transactions as selling an item for less than the tagged price. Also, there may be errors in record-keeping, such as failure to record markups or markdowns, markup cancellations, or customer returns. Additionally, some items are lost or damaged beyond repair. But the most alarming cause of shortage is theft by both employees and customers. This problem is so prevalent that stores anticipate shortages when formulating pricing policies.

Stores or departments with excessive shortages must make an attempt to isolate the prime reasons for this loss and begin a program that will ease the problem. Such programs may range from monitoring record-keeping to initiating anti-shoplifting campaigns.

To calculate the stock shortage figure, a way to monitor the amount of inventory on hand is required. The inventory figure obtained by actually counting and recording the retail price of all unsold items is known as the **physical or periodic inventory**. Another method is to record changes in the retail price such as markdowns, additional markups, markdown cancellations, and transfers of merchandise when they occur. This method is known as the **book or perpetual inventory**.

Book Inventory

The first step to determine the stock shortage is to calculate the book inventory. Book inventory is the initial inventory adjusted by the additional purchases, net sales, price changes (mainly markdowns), and employee discounts. When price changes are made on merchandise, these changes too must be recorded. Moreover, it is vital to correctly document any change made in the physical inventory. Whether the changes are added or subtracted from the beginning inventory depends on the nature of the transaction. Purchases, additional markups, and markdown cancellations increase the inventory while the other transactions such as net sales, markdowns, and employee discounts decrease the inventory. The common formula for calculating book inventory is beginning inventory plus purchases minus net sales, markdowns, and employee discounts, as illustrated in the following:

EQUATION 4.1

$$Book\ Inventory\ =\ Beg.\ Inv.\ +\ Purch.\ -\ Net\ Sales\ -\ MD\ -\ Empl.\ Disc.$$

Problem   The Varsity Styles Company records the following transactions:

Beginning Inventory	=	$20,500
Additional Purchases	=	$50,000
Net Sales	=	$35,000
Markdowns	=	$24,000
Employee Discounts	=	$ 500

What is the book inventory?

Solution $Book\ Inventory\ =\ Beg.\ Inv.\ +\ Purch.\ -\ Net\ Sales\ -\ MD\ -\ Disc.$

$$=\ \$20,500.00\ +\ \$50,000.00$$

$$-\ \$35,000.00\ -\ \$24,000.00\ -\ \$500.00$$

$$=\ \$11,000.00$$

Physical Inventory

Physical inventory is determined by an actual tabulation of the retail price on all items not yet sold. Therefore, physical inventory includes not only merchandise on the floor, but also in stock rooms, window displays, warehouses, and marking areas. Most retailers complete a physical inventory only once or twice a year due to time and cost restraints. Physical inventory can run smoothly if it is well organized by the buyer, department manager, or owner. If there is no plan, there is confusion and as a result, errors easily are made.

Initially, some stores begin with a plan of all the areas in the store that must be counted. Employees are then assigned to specific areas and responsibilities. This type of plan prevents areas from being overlooked. Before the actual count begins, merchandise should be arranged in an orderly, easily accessible fashion. Persons that are assigned to recording the inventory information (most frequently price, code numbers, and size) then thoroughly examine their entire designated area and record the necessary information. Working in teams of two will also help to speed up the process and reduce errors. Stores that are computerized may scan bar codes to capture the information. This process can save time and reduce recording errors. When the inventory sheets are collected, the unit prices are totalled to arrive at the physical inventory figure.

Dollar Shortage

When the result of a physical inventory is compared to that of a book inventory, one of three situations may arise. First, the book inventory may equal the physical inventory. This is an ideal situation but it rarely occurs. Second, the book inventory may be lower than the physical inventory. This situation is called a **stock overage** and generally is caused by mistakes in counting the physical inventory or in failure to record or correctly enter items in the book inventory. It may also be an indication of financial tampering. However, it is far more common to find the third situation in which the book inventory is higher than the physical inventory. The situation is called a stock or inventory shortage. This figure represents the disappearance or loss of merchandise in dollars or as a percentage of the net sales. The dollar stock shortage is simply the difference between the dollar book inventory and the dollar physical inventory as is illustrated in Equation 4.2:

EQUATION 4.2

$$\$Shortage = Book\ Inventory - Physical\ Inventory$$

Problem   Suppose the Varsity Styles Company mentioned in the previous problem on page 147 found their physical inventory to be $10,670. We found that the book inventory was $11,000. What was the dollar shortage?

Solution

$$\$Shortage = Book\ Inventory - Physical\ Inventory$$
$$= \$11,000.00 - \$10,670.00$$
$$= \$330.00$$

Shortage Percentage

Shortage frequently is given as a percentage of the net sales and is referred to as the **shortage percentage**. The percentage figure allows comparisons between stores that are similar in merchandise or sales volumes. The shortage percentage is multiplied by the net sales figure to obtain the dollar shortage, as shown in the following:

EQUATION 4.3

$$Shortage\ \% = \left(\frac{\$Shortage}{Net\ Sales}\right) 100\%$$

Problem   Returning again to the Varsity Styles Company example, what is the shortage percentage given net sales of $15,000 and a $330 shortage?

Solution
$$Shortage\ \% = \left(\frac{\$Shortage}{Net\ Sales} \right) 100\%$$

$$= \left(\frac{\$330.00}{\$15,000.00} \right) 100\%$$

$$= (.022)\ 100\%$$

$$= 2.2\%$$

Problem   Savemor Discount Store expects to find an 8% shortage on net sales of $31,700. What is the dollar amount of the shortage?

Solution
$$\$Shortage = \left(\frac{Shortage\%}{100\%} \right) Net\ Sales$$

$$= \left(\frac{8\%}{100\%} \right) \$31,700.00$$

$$= (.08)\ \$31,700.00$$

$$= \$2,536.00$$

Problem   The Nimble Thimble Specialty Store opened the six-month period from August 1 to January 31, with an inventory of $10,000. During the period, $3,000 in additional purchases resulted in sales amounting to $4,500, markdowns of $100, and employee discounts worth $50. The physical inventory on January 31 showed the store had $8,125 worth of stock. What is the percent stock shortage?

Solution   To solve this problem, go through the following three steps and use all three equations (that is, 4.1, 4.2, and 4.3) presented earlier in the chapter.

Step 1   Find the book inventory.

$$Book\ Inv. = Beg.\ Inv. + Purch. - Net\ Sales - MD - Disc.$$

$$= \$10,000.00 + \$3,000.00$$
$$- \$4,500.00 - \$100.00 - \$50.00$$

$$= \$8,350.00$$

Step 2   Find the dollar shortage.

$$\$Shortage = Book\ Inventory - Physical\ Inventory$$

$$= \$8,350.00 - \$8,125.00$$

$$= \$225.00$$

Step 3 Find the shortage percentage.

$$\$Shortage = \left(\frac{Shortage\%}{100\%} \right) Net\ Sales$$

$$Shortage\% = \left(\frac{\$Shortage}{Net\ Sales} \right) 100\%$$

$$= \left(\frac{\$225.00}{\$4,500.00} \right) 100\%$$

$$= (.05)\ 100\%$$

$$= 5\%$$

Computer Drill 17: Stock Shortage

Stock Shortage is the name of the computer program that generates three types of problems for this section of the text. The types of problems available are:

- *Book Inventory*
- *Dollar Shortage*
- *Shortage Percentage*

Assignments

1. The Adit Company records the following transactions:

Initial Inventory	$14,817.00
Additional Purchases	$ 4,939.00
Net Sales	$ 7,408.00
Markdowns	$ 740.00
Employee Discounts	$ 148.00

What is the book inventory?

2. The finance manager in Cody's Department Store finds that the book inventory is $16,502.00 and the physical inventory is $16,171.00. The shortage is $_____ ?

3. What is the percent shortage for The Loy Company, if the net sales are $18,978.00 and the shortage is $881.00?

4. If a department has the following figures for the six-month period from August 1–January 31:

Inventory August 1	$67,236.00
Purchases (At Retail)	$22,412.00
Net Sales	$33,618.00
Markdowns	$ 3,361.00
Employee Discounts	$ 672.00

The calculated book inventory is $_____ ?

5. Using information from the previous problem and knowing that the physical inventory is $49,917.00, consequently the amount of the stock shortage is $_____ ?

6. The Malloy Company opened the six-month period from July 1 to December 31 with an inventory of $32,486.00. During the period, $10,828.00 in additional purchases resulted in sales amounting to $16,243.00, markdowns worth $1,624.00, and employee discounts worth $324.00. The physical inventory on December 31 showed the store had $24,620.00 worth of stock. What is the stock shortage percent?

TURNOVER

After receiving the merchandise ordered, the buyer hopes the goods will be sold rapidly, thereby generating profits and more funds to invest in new merchandise. As a measure of how rapidly goods are being sold, a quantity can be calculated that is called **stock turnover** (often shortened to turnover or turn). This quantity indicates how many times during a given period, which is normally a year, the average retail stock has been converted into sales. Even though turnover is normally calculated on a yearly basis, it may be calculated on any such basis as daily, weekly, monthly, or seasonal. Mathematically, it is a simple matter to convert turnover from one time period to another. A yearly turnover would be twelve times a turnover calculated on a monthly basis or fifty-two times that calculated on a weekly basis. In practice, however, this is a risky approach because it does not take into account monthly or weekly variations. It means that we are using one month's or one week's data to make predictions about the rest of the year. Turnover calculated over a short period, such as daily or weekly, seldom provides an accurate measure on which to base decisions.

Turnover is an indicator of how efficiently a department or store is being run. A higher turnover is not necessarily a better turnover. A high turnover means that sales are high in relation to dollars invested in inventory and that the buyer has met customers needs and wants by stocking the right colors, sizes, and prices. It also means that the goods were ordered and delivered in time for the peak period of consumer demand. Often salespeople are more excited about showing new items and their enthusiasm is beneficial to sales. Because the goods are moving rapidly, they are less likely to become shopworn or soiled and the need for markdown is reduced. Insurance and taxes on stock are reduced as well as the cost of storage space. Customer interest is stimulated by new merchandise and they are less likely to become bored and look elsewhere for new merchandise. Additionally, if the customers know that merchandise moves rapidly in the store they are less likely to wait for sales before making purchases.

In spite of all of these benefits, the turnover can become too high. Because turnover is an indicator of efficiency, a large turnover may indicate poor ordering habits. Too much reordering can increase transportation and clerical costs and can cause a company to lose out on the quantity discounts available for placing large orders. Sales also may be lost when items are not in stock, especially such basic necessities as hosiery and toiletries.

Stock Turnover At Retail

There are three bases on which to calculate stock turnover. The base used depends on the method of inventory, be it retail, cost, or units of merchandise. Because most stores now use the retail method of inventory, retail figures are the most popular basis to calculate stock turnover. When the retail method is used, stock turnover is the ratio of net sales to the average retail dollars invested in stock, as illustrated in the following equation:

EQUATION 4.4

$$Stock\ Turnover = \frac{\$Net\ Sales}{Average\ Stock\ at\ \$Retail}$$

Problem   During the month of June the home accessories department realized sales of $7,000. The average stock was $35,000 at retail. What is the stock turnover at retail for the month of June?

Solution
$$Stock\ turnover = \frac{\$Net\ Sales}{Average\ Stock\ at\ \$Retail}$$

$$= \frac{\$7,000.00}{\$35,000.00}$$

$$= 0.2$$

Problem   The new manager of a sport specialty shop finds old records that indicate that the net sales for the previous year were $200,000 and that the stock turnover at retail was 2. What was the average dollar investment in stock?

Solution
$$Average\ Stock = \frac{\$Net\ Sales}{Stock\ Turnover}$$

$$= \frac{\$200,000.00}{2.0}$$

$$= \$100,000.00$$

Problem   The yearly stock turn goal for a maternity clothing and accessories store is 4. The average dollar stock for the year was $111,000. Find the net sales for the year.

Solution
$$\$Net\ Sales = (Stock\ Turnover)\ Average\ Stock$$

$$= (4.0)\ \$111,000.00$$

$$= \$444,000.00$$

Stock Turnover At Cost

Those stores that record merchandising figures at cost calculate stock turnover based on cost. Stock turnover based on cost is the ratio of the cost of the goods sold to the average cost of the stock. This is demonstrated in the following formula:

EQUATION 4.5

$$Stock\ Turnover = \frac{Cost\ of\ Goods\ Sold}{Average\ Stock\ at\ \$Cost}$$

Problem   The gourmet department realized $28,000 in sales for the month of February. The merchandise originally cost $18,000. If the average retail stock was $9,700 at retail and $6,000 at cost, what was the stock turnover at cost?

Solution

$$Stock\ Turnover = \frac{Cost\ of\ Goods\ Sold}{Average\ Cost\ of\ \$Stock}$$

$$= \frac{\$18,000.00}{\$6,000.00}$$

$$= 3.0$$

Stock Turnover in Units of Merchandise

Inventory records can track the number of items within a specific subclassification or grouping and the stock turnover then can be based on the units of merchandise. For example, consumers often purchase multiple tops or blouses to go with bottoms or pants and skirts. Therefore, by analyzing turnover using units the retailer is able to derive a ratio of tops to bottoms. If you sell three tops per bottom, your inventory investment should be comparable. The stock turnover in units is the ratio of the number of units sold to the average number of units in stock, as evidenced in the following:

EQUATION 4.6

$$Stock\ Turnover = \frac{Units\ Sold}{Average\ Stock\ in\ Units}$$

Problem   After a three-month period, Jennifer, the manager for cosmetics, wanted to re-examine some of the accessory items carried in her department. During this period, 30 cosmetic bags had been sold. The average stock on hand is 20. What is the unit stock turnover for the period?

Solution

$$Stock\ Turnover = \frac{Units\ Sold}{Average\ Stock\ in\ Units}$$

$$= \frac{30}{20}$$

$$= 1.5$$

Calculating the Average Stock Figure

In the previous problems the average dollar retail was given, which simplified the problems because in real life, generally, you will have to calculate the average stock. A simple way to find the average stock is to record the stock at the beginning and end of a period. This can be done in retail, cost, or unit figures. The average then is calculated by adding the beginning and ending numbers and dividing the sum by two.

A stock average that is done for a year overlooks seasonal, monthly, and weekly variations. A stock average based on beginning and ending inventory figures for the year will give an estimate that is too low for some periods and too high for others. A more accurate course of action would be to include seasonal or monthly figures. The average stock at retail, cost, or units is calculated by using seasonal or monthly periods.

An average for a year could be based on a beginning monthly figure, an ending monthly figure, and figures for each month or season for equally spaced intermediate periods. This sum then is divided by the number of terms included in the sum.

Therefore, a stock average for the year will have thirteen figures, one for each beginning inventory and one for the ending inventory of the last month. The ending inventory figure is necessary to include in order to reflect the sales and stock activity that took place during the month. This sum would be divided by thirteen, which is the number of factors used in the equation. This calculation is shown in the following formula:

EQUATION 4.7

$$Average\ Stock = \frac{(Beg.\ +\ Inter.\ 1\ +\ Inter.\ 2\ +\ Inter.\ N\ +\ End)}{\#Terms\ in\ Sum}$$

Problem The Happy Hunter Sports Shop recorded the following seasonal figures:

Inventory (At Cost)

February 1	$ 8,000.00
June 1	$10,000.00
October 1	$11,000.00
January 31	$ 9,000.00

What would be the average stock for the year of the Happy Hunter Sports Shop?

Solution

$$Aver.\ Stock\ at\ Cost = \frac{(Beg.\ +\ Inter.\ 1\ +\ Inter.\ 2\ +\ End)}{\#Terms\ in\ Sum}$$

$$= \frac{(\$8,000.00\ +\ \$10,000.00\ +\ \$11,000.00\ +\ \$9,000.00)}{4}$$

$$= \frac{\$38,000.00}{4}$$

$$= \$9,500.00$$

Problem Bernie's Department Store records sales and inventory monthly. The inventory is recorded both at retail and at cost. Cost of goods sold for the period was $15,500.

		$ Inventory	
	Retail $Sales	At Retail	At Cost
January 3	2,000	4,000	3,000
February 2	2,000	3,000	2,000
March 2	1,000	6,000	5,000
April 3	2,000	5,000	4,000
May 2	1,000	5,000	4,000
June 2	1,000	5,000	4,000
July 1	2,000	3,000	2,000
August 2	1,000	5,000	4,000
September 4	2,000	7,000	6,000
October 2	2,000	6,000	5,000
November 3	1,000	4,000	3,000
December 1	3,000	4,000	3,000
January		8,000	7,000

What is the stock turnover at retail for the year?

Solution
$$Stock\ Turnover\ at\ Retail = \frac{\$Net\ Sales}{Average\ Stock\ at\ \$Retail}$$

Step 1 Calculate net sales (the sum of all the sales for the period).

$$
\begin{aligned}
Net\ Sales\ = \quad &\$\ 2,000.00 \\
+ \quad &2,000.00 \\
+ \quad &1,000.00 \\
+ \quad &2,000.00 \\
+ \quad &1,000.00 \\
+ \quad &1,000.00 \\
+ \quad &2,000.00 \\
+ \quad &1,000.00 \\
+ \quad &2,000.00 \\
+ \quad &2,000.00 \\
+ \quad &1,000.00 \\
+ \quad &\underline{3,000.00} \\
= \quad &\$20,000.00
\end{aligned}
$$

Step 2 Find the average stock at retail.

$$Aver.\ Stock\ at\ Ret.\ = \frac{(Beg.\ +\ Inter.\ 1\ +\ Inter.\ N\ +\ End)}{\#Terms\ in\ Sum}$$

First, add all the monthly retail sales inventory figures.

$$
\begin{aligned}
\quad &\$\ 4,000.00 \\
+ \quad &3,000.00 \\
+ \quad &6,000.00 \\
+ \quad &5,000.00 \\
+ \quad &5,000.00 \\
+ \quad &5,000.00 \\
+ \quad &3,000.00 \\
+ \quad &5,000.00 \\
+ \quad &7,000.00 \\
+ \quad &6,000.00 \\
+ \quad &4,000.00 \\
+ \quad &4,000.00 \\
+ \quad &\underline{8,000.00} \\
= \quad &\$65,000.00
\end{aligned}
$$

Then, divide the sum by the number of factors used in the equation.

$$\frac{\$65,000.00}{13} = \$5,000.00$$

Step 3 Find the stock turnover.

$$Stock\ Turnover\ at\ Retail = \frac{\$Net\ Sales}{Average\ Stock\ at\ \$Retail}$$

$$= \frac{\$20,000.00}{\$5,000.00}$$

$$= 4.0$$

Problem   Given the information in the previous problem, what is the yearly stock turnover at cost for Bernie's Department Store?

Solution $$Stock\ Turnover\ at\ Cost = \frac{Cost\ of\ Goods\ Sold}{Average\ Stock\ at\ \$Cost}$$

Step 1 Cost of goods sold is the sum of all the sales at cost for the period. In this problem the figure is given. Cost of goods sold = $15,500.00.

Step 2 Find the average stock at cost.

$$Aver.\ Stock\ at\ Cost = \frac{(Beg.\ +\ Inter.\ 1\ +\ Inter.\ N\ +\ End)}{\#Terms\ in\ Sum}$$

First, add all the monthly cost inventory figures.

$$
\begin{array}{rr}
 & \$\ 3,000.00 \\
+ & 2,000.00 \\
+ & 5,000.00 \\
+ & 4,000.00 \\
+ & 4,000.00 \\
+ & 4,000.00 \\
+ & 2,000.00 \\
+ & 4,000.00 \\
+ & 6,000.00 \\
+ & 5,000.00 \\
+ & 3,000.00 \\
+ & 3,000.00 \\
+ & \underline{7,000.00} \\
= & \$52,000.00
\end{array}
$$

Then, divide the sum by the number of factors used in the equation.

$$= \frac{\$52,000.00}{13}$$

$$= \$4,000.00$$

Step 3 Find the stock turnover at cost.

$$Stock\ Turnover\ at\ Cost = \frac{Cost\ of\ Goods\ Sold}{Average\ Stock\ at\ \$Cost}$$

$$= \frac{\$15,500.00}{\$4,000.00}$$

$$= 3.875$$

Problem Each month the Bab-Pad Company records the sales and opening and closing inventories.

	$Sales	$Opening Inventory	$Closing Inventory
February	56,000	106,000	125,000
March	60,000	125,000	110,000
April	52,000	110,000	110,000
May	50,000	110,000	94,000
June	40,000	94,000	76,000
July	39,000	76,000	72,000

What is the six-month stock turnover for the period?

Solution

$$Stock\ Turnover = \frac{\$Net\ Sales}{Average\ Stock\ at\ \$Retail}$$

Step 1 Find the net sales for the period.

$$Net\ Sales = Sum\ of\ Sales\ for\ Period$$

$$
\begin{aligned}
&\$56,000.00 \\
+\ &60,000.00 \\
+\ &52,000.00 \\
+\ &50,000.00 \\
+\ &40,000.00 \\
+\ &\underline{39,000.00} \\
=\ &\$297,000.00
\end{aligned}
$$

Step 2 Find the average stock for the period.

$$Aver.\ Stock = \frac{(Beg. + Inter.\ 1 + Inter.\ N + End)}{Number\ of\ Terms\ in\ Sum}$$

First, add all the monthly opening inventory figures.

$$
\begin{aligned}
&\$106,000.00 \\
+\ &125,000.00 \\
+\ &110,000.00 \\
+\ &110,000.00 \\
+\ &94,000.00 \\
+\ &76,000.00 \\
+\ &\underline{72,000.00} \\
=\ &\$693,000.00
\end{aligned}
$$

Then, divide the sum by the number of factors used in the equation.

$$\frac{\$693,000.00}{7} = \$99,000.00$$

Step 3 Find the stock turnover at retail (see *equation 4.4*).

$$Stock\ Turnover\ at\ Retail = \frac{\$Net\ Sales}{Average\ Stock\ at\ \$Retail}$$

$$= \frac{\$297,000.00}{\$99,000.00}$$

$$= 3.0$$

Stock Turnover for the Whole Store

Calculating the stock turnover for an entire store can be solved by using individual department turnover information. The net sales figure for each department is divided by the department stock turnover to obtain the average stock figures. The stock turn for the store is the sum of the net sales for each department divided by the sum of the average stock in each department, as shown in the following:

EQUATION 4.8

$$Stock\ Turn\ for\ Whole = \frac{Net\ Sales\ 1\ +\ Net\ Sales\ 2\ +\ Net\ Sales\ N}{Avg.\ Stock\ 1\ +\ Avg.\ Stock\ 2\ +\ Avg.\ Stock\ N}$$

Problem   During the past year, Strawberry Girl, a teenage specialty shop, recorded the following information for each of its four departments.

Department	$Net Sales	Stock Turnover
Jewelry	4,000.00	2.5
Sportswear	12,000.00	5.0
Dresses	16,000.00	4.0
Lingerie & Sleepwear	8,000.00	4.0

What is the yearly stock turnover for the store? (Please note that in this problem the average stock is not given, and must be calculated for each department.)

Solution   Find the sum of the net sales for each department. Then, calculate the average stock for each department and find the sum of the average stock figures.

$$Stock\ Turnover = \frac{Net\ Sales\ 1\ +\ Net\ Sales\ 2\ +\ Net\ Sales\ 3\ +\ Net\ Sales\ 4}{Avg.\ Stock\ 1\ +\ Avg.\ Stock\ 2\ +\ Avg.\ Stock\ 3\ +\ Avg.\ Stock\ 4}$$

Jewelry $= \$\ 4,000.00 \div 2.5 = \$1,600.00$

Sportswear $= \$12,000.00 \div 5.0 = \$2,400.00$

Dresses $= \$16,000.00 \div 4.0 = \$4,000.00$

Lingerie $= \dfrac{\$8,000.00 \div 4.0}{\$40,000.00} = \dfrac{\$\ 2,000.00}{\$10,000.00}$

$$= \frac{\$40,000.00}{\$10,000.00}$$

$$= 4.0$$

Capital Turnover

Capital turnover is the ratio of net sales to average stock at cost. The calculations for capital turnover are similar to those for stock turnover except the net sales figure is divided by the average stock at cost. Although merchandisers usually find the stock turnover to be more useful, auditors and investors prefer to know the capital turnover because it more accurately reflects the relationship between dollars invested at sales generated. Financial statements usually supply this information because sales and stock figures have been recorded at cost. The capital turnover will always be larger than the stock turnover because the net sales always will be divided by a smaller average stock figure because the average cost figure is always smaller than the average retail figure. The calculation for capital turnover is illustrated in the following:

EQUATION 4.9

$$Capital\ Turnover = \frac{\$Net\ Sales}{Average\ Stock\ at\ \$Cost}$$

Problem Dandy Dan's had an average inventory at cost of $28,000 and net sales of $148,000 for the past year. What was the yearly capital turnover?

Solution

$$Capital\ Turnover = \frac{\$Net\ Sales}{Average\ Stock\ at\ \$Cost}$$

$$= \frac{\$148,000.00}{\$28,000.00}$$

$$= 5.29$$

Computer Drill 18: Turnover

Turnover is the name of the computer program that generates six types of problems for this section of the text. The types of problems available are:

- *Stock Turnover at Retail*
- *Stock Turnover at Cost*
- *Stock Turnover in Units of Merchandise*
- *Calculating the Average Stock Figure*
- *Stock Turnover for the Whole Store*
- *Capital Turnover*

Assignments

1. An inventory of $740.00 at cost was recorded for the Candy Department on January 2. The cost of the merchandise sold during the month was $3,700.00 at cost. What is the stock turnover at cost?

2. Total retail sales for the year in the Kotz Boutique were $9,100.00. The capital turnover was 7.0. What was the average stock at cost?

3. The average stock at retail for the Health Food Department was $1,950.00 and the stock turn at retail for the year was 6.0. What were the net sales for the period?

4. An inventory of $1,530.00 at retail was recorded for the Western Wear Department on February 4. The cost of the merchandise sold during the month was $4,590.00 at retail. What is the stock turnover at retail?

5. Sarita and Son's had an average inventory at cost of $1,140.00 and net sales of $7,980.00 for the past year. What was the yearly capital turnover?

6. The Erie Store records inventory and sales every four months:

	$ Inventory		$ Sales At Cost
	At Retail	At Cost	
Jan. 2, 1994	1,100.00	710.00	1,500.00
May 3, 1994	1,240.00	790.00	1,590.00
Sept. 2, 1994	1,240.00	750.00	1,530.00
Jan. 2, 1995	1,320.00	830.00	

What is the stock turnover at cost for the period?

7. During the past year, The Detail Shop recorded the following information for each of its three departments.

Department	$Net Sales	Stock Turnover
Dresses	$2,083.00	5.3
Lingerie	$1,837.00	3.7
Jewelry	$1,820.00	1.8

What is the yearly stock turnover for the whole store?

8. The cutlery department sold 5,680 items of merchandise during the year just ended. If the average stock was 710 items, what was the stock turn in units of merchandise?

STOCK-SALES RATIO

In the previous section, you learned that the average stock on hand is calculated as the ratio of the net sales to the stock turnover, but this figure does not indicate how much stock should be on hand during the next time period. The **stock-sales ratio** provides us with one way to calculate how much stock is needed for sales during a specified period that is usually one month. Stock-sales ratios are calculated using beginning-of-the-month figures (BOM) or ending-of-the-month figures (EOM). The **BOM stock-sales ratio** shows how much stock is needed during the month. The **EOM stock-sales-ratio** can be used to determine performance during the month or to find a stock figure for the following month. The EOM stock figure of one month is always equivalent to the BOM stock for the following month.

A stock-sales ratio of three would mean that an inventory of $90,000 must be on hand to meet sales needs of $30,000 ($90,000 ÷ $30,000 = 3). This figure is then compared with previous figures to determine if greater stock efficiency has been achieved. If a retailer can generate an equivalent sales volume with a lower investment in inventory, then the business operation should be operating more efficiently.

BOM Stock-Sales Ratio

The BOM stock-sales ratio is found by dividing the stock on hand at the beginning of the month by planned sales for the same time period. (See *Chapter 5* for discussion of planned sales.) It is the most frequently used method of calculating stock-sales ratio and the initials BOM often are omitted and the quantity simply is called the stock-sales ratio. The following formula illustrates the calculation:

EQUATION 4.10

$$BOM\ Stock\text{-}Sales\ Ratio = \frac{BOM\ Stock}{\$Sales}$$

Problem For the month of May, a buyer had an opening inventory of $216,000 and planned sales totaling $120,000. What is the stock-sales ratio?

Solution
$$BOM\ Stock\text{-}Sales\ Ratio = \frac{BOM\ Stock}{\$Sales}$$

$$= \frac{\$216,000.00}{\$120,000.00}$$

$$= 1.8$$

Problem From previous experience, the buyer for the housewares department estimates that the stock-sales ratio for the month of March will be 4.2 and there should be approximately $37,500 worth of sales. At the beginning of the month, how much stock should the department have on hand?

Solution

$$BOM\ Stock\ =\ (BOM\ Stock\text{-}Sales\ Ratio)\ \$Sales$$

$$=\ (4.2)\ \$37,500.00$$

$$=\ \$157,500.00$$

Problem A children's shoe store has an opening inventory of $16,500 and expects a 2.2 stock-sales ratio during June. What are the expected sales?

Solution

$$Sales\ =\ BOM\ Stock\ \div\ BOM\ Stock\text{-}Sales\ Ratio$$

$$=\ (\$16,500.00)\ \div\ 2.2$$

$$=\ \$7,500.00$$

EOM Stock-Sales Ratio

The formula for the EOM stock-sales ratio is similar to that for BOM ratio except that the end of the month stock figure is divided by the actual sales for the month. The EOM ratio sometimes is used in planning for the following month. But it is really only meaningful if the sales for the following month remain unchanged. This formula is stated as follows:

EQUATION 4.11

$$EOM\ Stock\text{-}Sales\ Ratio\ =\ \frac{EOM\ Stock}{\$Sales}$$

Problem The assistant manager of Horace's Fashion Apparel notes that the sportswear department has recorded a monthly opening inventory of $93,150 and a closing inventory of $82,800, with a corresponding $34,500 in sales. What was the department's end of the month stock-sales ratio?

Solution

$$EOM\ Stock\text{-}Sales\ Ratio\ =\ \frac{EOM\ stock}{\$Sales}$$

$$=\ \frac{\$82,800.00}{\$34,500.00}$$

$$=\ 2.4$$

Computer Drill 19: Stock-Sales Ratio

Stock-Sales Ratio is the name of the computer program that generates two types of problems for this section of the text. The types of problems available are:

- *BOM Stock-Sales Ratio*
- *EOM Stock-Sales Ratio*

Assignments

1. The small appliances department had a BOM stock for the month of October amounting to $119,880.00. The sales for the month were $14,800.00. What was the department's BOM stock-sales ratio?

2. During the month of February, a boutique owner is aiming for a stock-sales ratio of 1.9. Given a beginning stock of $42,940.00, what should be the sales for February to meet this goal?

3. The Bed and Bath Department has planned sales of $29,700.00 for the month of September and would like to obtain a stock-sales ratio of 1.9. How much stock must be on hand as of September 1?

4. The Boot Department began the month of November with a BOM stock of $53,970.00. On November 20th, sales for the department were $20,560.00. To obtain a stock-sales ratio of 2.1, how much more must be sold in the department by the end of the month?

5. The Sane Company is planning to begin the month of June with $75,110.00 of stock and would like to obtain $20,300.00 in sales. What is the company's planned stock-sales ratio?

6. A buyer is trying to decrease the infant department's stock-sales ratio to 3.7. The projected sales figure for August is $3,000.00. To meet this goal, how much stock must be on hand?

CHAPTER FIVE

Planning Merchandising Budgets

The primary responsibility of a store buyer is to maintain an inventory that meets customer needs and wants within the financial guidelines set by management. Through the merchandise planning process the buyer tries to balance inventory and sales to achieve this goal. The financial tool that retailers use to determine the dollar value of an estimated inventory is the **six-month merchandising plan**.

It is essential for the retailer to have enough inventory on hand to meet customer demands. Inventory represents a sizeable investment that must be aggressively monitored and controlled if profits are to be generated. The retailer must balance carefully the anticipated sales against the stock on hand and the stock to be purchased. This involves planning a budget with projections based on previous merchandising activities. The plan covers a specific period of time. It is common for the year to be divided into two six-month periods, such as February 1 to July 31 and August 1 to January 31. The starting months usually correspond to periods when stock is at a minimum. For instance, inventory tends to be lowest after the heavy Christmas sales and before stocking for back-to-school and fall promotions.

Budget planning is an on-going process that constantly needs to be reassessed. Six-month merchandising plans include projections for sales, inventory, markdowns, and markups. The plan can be adjusted as trends change. Because merchandise must be on hand to avoid lost sales, stores do not wait until all inventory is sold before ordering more stock. Thus, six-month plans are often broken down into smaller monthly planning periods. The same planning can be used for February through July or August through January by crossing out the months at the top of the columns that are not under consideration. Figure 5.1 shows a typical six-month merchandising plan form.

To establish a rational and agreeable merchandising plan, input should come from all levels of personnel, that is, merchandise managers, department managers, and buyers. This input should be considered and discussed before the plan has been finalized. There are three basic approaches that may be taken to planning merchandising budgets. These three methods are: 1) top-down planning; 2) bottom-up planning; and 3) a combination of top-down and bottom-up. In top-down planning, management establishes an overall sales goal that subsequently is segmented into departmental goals. The bottom-up plan allows each department to establish a goal and then these departmental plans are merged to establish an overall sales plan for the entire retail establishment. Sometimes a combination of both the bottom-up and top-down methods are used to develop a mutually feasible plan.

FIGURE 5.1

The Six-Month Merchandising Plan

Season: _____ Year: _____

Department Name: _____ #: _____

		LAST YEAR	PLAN FOR THIS PERIOD	ACTUAL
Gross Margin$ (Ch. 1 & 6)				
%				
Operating Expenses (Ch. 6)				
Operating Profit (Ch. 6)				
Cash Discount% (Ch. 3)				
Allowable MD% (Ch. 2)				
Shortage% (Ch. 4)				
Season Turnover (Ch. 4)				
Discount% (Ch. 2)				

		FEB AUG	MAR SEPT	APR OCT	MAY NOV	JUNE DEC	JULY JAN	TOTAL
Sales$ (Ch. 5)	Last Year$							
	Plan$							
	Actual$							
	Variation%							
Sales Transactions (Ch. 5)	#Last Year's Transactions							
	#Plan Transactions							
	Variation%							
	Adjusted Plan							
Retail Stock BOM$ (Ch. 5)	Last Year							
	Planned							
	Actual							
	Adjusted Plan							
Markdowns (Ch. 2 & 5)	Last Year$							
	%Total Last Year							
	Planned$							
	%Total Planned							
	Actual$							
	%Total Actual Sales							
Purchases Retail$ (Ch. 1)	Last Year							
	Planned							
	Actual							
	Adjusted Plan							
Purchases Cost$ (Ch. 5)	Last Year							
	Planned							
	Actual							
	Adjusted Plan							
Markup (Ch. 1)	Maintained (Last Year$)							
	%							
	Initial (Planned$)							
	%							
	Cumulative (Actual $)							
	%							

Best Resources   Name   Terms   Lines
1.
2.
3.

Buyer _____ Merchandise Manager _____ Controller _____

Remarks:

It is best to be realistic rather than idealistic when developing the six-month merchandising plan. Because these plans often are thought of as goals, and frequently serve as a means of determining performance levels, it would be very disappointing for a buyer or a department to receive a low performance rating because the ideal goals set in an unrealistic plan were not met—especially if realistic goals were surpassed. The merchandising plan should include all of the information necessary to arrive at sound decision making and should not include information that is useless or vague. While the intermediate components of the merchandising plan may vary, the primary items are: sales, reductions, stock, and purchases. These components will be covered in more detail in the following sections. Additionally, the format of a merchandising plan can be revamped or reorganized to suit the needs of the department most effectively.

The six-month merchandising plan takes on added dimension when its components are examined separately. The merchandising plan illustrated in Figure 5.1 has corresponding chapter numbers (in parenthesis) that will help you to refer to those specific chapters for relevant information relating to each area on the plan. Some of the information presented in the six-month merchandising plan, such as gross margin and operating expenses, are obtained from the profit and loss statement. The profit and loss statement generally is calculated by upper management and reflects the store as a whole. Alternatively, it can be calculated by a department manager to reflect that single department's status. An explanation of how the figures on a profit and loss statement are derived is provided in *Chapter Six*.

PLANNING SALES

The object of planning is to arrive at fair and logical projections for the period after all available facts and information are considered. **Planned sales**, the first step in developing a merchandising plan, is a forecast or prediction of sales volume. A planned sales figure that is illogical or impractical can distort the merchandising plan and even affect your evaluation as a buyer or manager because a plan that projects unrealistically high sales that are not attained can make a department appear to be selling below capacity.

Accurate and realistic sales predictions are basic and vital to profitable planning. When projecting sales volume, an analysis of past records is very beneficial. From these past records the buyer can gain insight based on prior sales history. These records also provide a baseline for balanced inventory levels. When no previous records are available, as would be the case with a new store, a wise buyer or retailer will seek out other non-competing stores of similar size, merchandise, and quality to see what information those stores might be willing to share. Although no two stores are identical, the comparisons that occur from shared data and information will bring you closer to a realistic perspective. Data from various trade and professional organizations also will prove helpful.

Statements made in trade association journals and business magazines will assist the buyer not only in understanding the general economic forecast, but in knowing more about specific product acceptance based on general consumer attitudes. When assimilating what you read, be aware of percentage changes over a specific period of time and also the rate of change. When given a percentage figure, you should always ask: "Percentage of what?" and "Over what period of time?"

When forecasting a sales plan, a buyer should be aware of a variety of indicators, which will help predict a change in sales level. Not all departments, stores, or cities have the same conditions that influence customers. However, there are some general predictors that should be monitored and taken into consideration before finalizing a sales plan. Because planned sales are determined in a subjective manner based on past sales figures, current events, trends, and personal judgement, some incongruity between planned sales and actual sales should be anticipated. Several variables may be altered or others may intervene that were not anticipated, thus affecting anticipated sales. For example, if a new line of goods is accepted much more readily than anticipated, sales may increase beyond the planned figure. On the other hand, increased competition or an inability to meet demand for a product may cause sales to fall below the plan.

The factors that act upon sales volume may be classified as either external or internal in nature. External causes include such elements as the local economy, the weather, ecological issues, and consumer tastes. An external cause is any important event that influences people in the community and alters the prevailing purchasing patterns either financially, physically, or psychologically. Some specific examples of external factors are:

1. A layoff of large proportion certainly would affect the local economy by reducing the amount of money consumers have to spend. If this situation is extended for a long period of time, other businesses also may be influenced adversely. Consumer attitudes may be altered, which in turn could influence consumer spending patterns or the price levels at which these customers are purchasing.

2. A flu epidemic certainly would produce a change in sales by keeping people at home, either because they are sick or because they do not want to be exposed to germs.

3. Climatic changes, whether too hot, too cold, or too wet also tend to alter customer consumption. Generally, people prefer to stay where it is comfortable rather than brave the elements. Such acts of nature as floods or high winds may cause major physical damage to buildings and streets, which not only alters consumer behavior, but may temporarily or even permanently close businesses.

4. Local population trends such as the size and location of the population are also important considerations over which a buyer or retailer has little control. As more industries move into an area, the size of the population will increase as more jobs become available and, subsequently, sales will increase as there are more people with money to spend. Unfortunately, the opposite also is true. When factories and businesses close, people lose jobs and may have to move to obtain work. Even if the populace doesn't dwindle, spending will be tight until the situation is alleviated.

5. Location, transportation, and parking have a major impact on consumer traffic and spending. If people can reach a location with ease, frustration is reduced and the shopping experience is more enjoyable. Gasoline shortages may adversely affect retail sales in the suburbs, while bus strikes or crime rates may deter inner-city shoppers. Many stores in the inner cities have been forced to abandon deteriorating neighborhoods. It is very advantageous to have a business located in an area surrounded by other successful

businesses. Additionally, locating near stores with comparable merchandise will attract customers who are interested in comparison shopping. Of course, too much competition in one location would saturate the market causing the opposite effect.

6. Political and social events that result in increased spending or growth are additional examples of external effects. Such social occasions as sporting events, conventions, dances, and balls stimulate consumer buying. However, it should be kept in mind that such events also may take money out of the local economy. For example, football fans who go to Hawaii for a pre-Christmas football game take thousands of dollars away from the local economy at a time when sales are very important to local retailers. On the other hand, such political events as tax decreases or rebates have a stimulating impact. Even news coverage that discusses the possibility of such events can cause public reaction.

7. Another external factor would be a change in consumer taste or acceptance. For example, cosmetic sales have been stimulated greatly by the development of more scents and colognes for men. Another example is the public's acceptance of the promotion of intimate apparel. Because of this change in attitude, companies now have greater freedom in presenting their merchandise, which has increased the sales potential substantially. Additionally, sales in one category may rise while those in another decline. When blue jeans became popular, sales of sportswear zoomed while sales of dresses decreased. As the sales of turtlenecks and sport shirts increased, the sales of neckties decreased in many stores. Other trends have become apparent only over a greater span of time. For example, the average man's investment in business suits gradually declined when separates, mix and match, and coordinate groupings began to gain acceptance within the business community.

A retailer has little control over most external causes or trends. On the other hand, a retailer has some measure of control over internal factors. Internal factors include operational policies and procedures that are controlled by management. These policy and procedure changes generally are made with the assumption that overall sales volume will increase. Some internal effects are:

1. Store expansion, renovation, or an upgrade of the store's fashion image, such as adding a higher-priced line of merchandise. This will attract customers who will want to see the new or renovated store, or who are interested in a higher or lower price line.

2. A change in advertising policy or promotional plans may provide the additional emphasis needed to increase sales. A full page advertisement in the middle of summer to announce "Lemon Days" can bring shoppers out despite the heat. Other promotional events include Anniversary Day Sales, Founder's Day Sales, Back-to-School Sales, Storewide Clearance Sales, or End-of-Year Sales.

3. As part of good promotional planning, more dramatic, visually stimulating approaches may be taken in store windows. Displays that are intriguing and captivate the eye are quite effective. For example, Bloomingdale's unique

approach to store windows in 1976 introduced the use of unexpected, typically life-like scenes, such as the local sauna and the dressing room as settings for fashion display. Because this had not been done before, several media sources covered it as if it was a news event. Such attention from the media gave the store unanticipated, free advertising across the country and was very advantageous for sales.

4. The use of catalogs, direct mailings, trunk showings, and customer services can also stimulate sales. Customer services may include low-cost gift wrapping, free parking, child care facilities, delivery services, free alterations, package check facilities, and personal shopping or fashion consulting.

In addition to internal and external factors that impact planning, the retailer also must adjust for the number of merchandising days in the year. When planning sales it is important for the retailer to take into account the number of selling days and to be aware of the potential impact of major holidays. The retailer may decide to increase store hours by staying open later in the evening or may close for the day to give employees more time to be with family members.

Due to the yearly changes in trends, number of selling days, and when holidays are acknowledged, sales history information can be very valuable. One of the most efficient ways to keep track of sales trends is to record the number of transactions and dollar sales in conjunction with the corresponding calendar dates. Information regarding events that alter purchasing impulses, such as weather conditions, special promotions, holidays, and changes in store policy also should be recorded. In other words, it is useful to compile a daily sales record or log with a listing of all relevant external and internal factors. This data often is entered in a book called "Beat Last Year". The book gets its name from the object of the challenge, which is to top the previous year's sales. The format of the "Beat Last Year" book is easy to organize (see *Figure 5.2*). Some of the same information also can be tracked and analyzed by computer.

Please note: when calculating weekly totals at the beginning of the month, the week seldom runs from Sunday through Saturday. If the first of the month falls on Thursday there are only four (or less) selling days in that week. Therefore, the weekly totals may appear below average. This distortion may be corrected by including daily totals for Monday through Wednesday of the previous month. A weekly total that utilizes sales from a previous month cannot be used to calculate the monthly total. The monthly total is found by adding only those sales achieved during each day of the month.

FIGURE 5.2

Example of "Beat Last Year" Format

Month: _____ 20 ____

Day	Date	Total Sales	# Trans.	Relevant Factors
Monday				
Tuesday	1			
Wednesday	2			
Thursday	3			
Friday	4			
Saturday	5			
Sunday	6			
Week				
Monday	7			
Tuesday	8			
Wednesday	9			
Thursday	10			
Friday	11			
Saturday	12			
Sunday	13			
Week				
Monday	14			
Tuesday	15			
Wednesday	16			
Thursday	17			
Friday	18			
Saturday	19			
Sunday	20			
Week				
Monday	21			
Tuesday	22			
Wednesday	23			
Thursday	24			
Friday	25			
Saturday	26			
Sunday	27			
Week				
Monday	28			
Tuesday	29			
Wednesday	30			
Thursday	31			
Friday				
Saturday				
Sunday				
Week				
Monday				
Tuesday				
Wednesday				
Thursday				
Friday				
Saturday				
Sunday				
Week				
Month				
Year-to-Date				

The "Beat Last Year" books or data bases from previous years are helpful in preparing the sales portion of the merchandising plan. This information provides a comparison of the number of transactions and sales volume in light of the number of selling days. Relevant factors that affected sales might be brought to mind and provide for stronger forecasting.

It is customary for the sales portion of the six-month merchandising plan to be broken down into months. Each month has five parts: last year's sales, planned sales, adjusted planned sales, actual sales, and the percentage variation from planned sales. The monthly sales total for last year may be calculated by using figures from the "Beat Last Year" book. The planned sales are those forecasted by the buyer and merchandise manager. When actual sales figures become available they are entered on the six-month plan. Whenever the actual sales are running substantially ahead or behind the planned sales, the buyer should adjust the plan by increasing or decreasing adjusted planned sales to reflect the situation. This creates an entry called **adjusted planned sales**, which will help prevent the store from being overstocked or understocked with inventory.

Planning Sales with Stable Prices

When prices, demand, and supply remain stable, last year's sales volume is a good estimate of this year's planned sales. However, this is a static approach to retailing and probably is not realistic. Also, it usually is more profitable to plan for increased sales. This means that instead of using the exact figures for last year, we use increased percentages to project the total sales. We also can look at sales by month as a percent of total sales. For example, if the month of May accounted for 10% of sales during the first six-month period last year, then it is reasonable to project that it will account for around 10% of the sales during the same period for the coming year. The planned sales for a specified month equals the monthly percentage of total sales accounted for in the month times the total planned sales, as shown below:

Monthly Planned Sales = (Monthly %) Total Planned Sales

Equation 5.1 can be used to calculate monthly planned sales when overall sales for the period are expected to change and the percentage of sales accounted for in one month is either stable or changing. This formula allows you to account for projected changes for the month and the total planning period simultaneously. The total planned sales can be rewritten as the monthly percentage multiplied by 100%, plus the percentage variation in sales multiplied by last year's total sales, as illustrated in the formula:

EQUATION 5.1

$$\textbf{\textit{Mon. Pl. Sales}} = \textbf{\textit{Mon.\%}} \left(\frac{\textbf{100\% + \$Sales Var.\%}}{\textbf{100\%}} \right) \textbf{\textit{LY Total \$Sales}}$$

Problem   The buyer for Gotham's Boutique expects an 8% increase in sales over last year's volume of $195,000. Last year, 14% of the sales occurred during November. Predict the planned sales for the coming November.

Solution

$$Nov.\ Pl.\ Sales = Mon.\% \left(\frac{100\% + \$Sales\ Var.\%}{100\%} \right) LY\ Total\ \$Sales$$

$$= 14\% \left(\frac{100\% + 8\%}{100\%} \right) \$195,000.00$$

$$= .14\ (1.08)\ (\$195,000.00)$$

$$= .14\ (\$210,600.00)$$

$$= \$29,484.00$$

Problem   Webster, Inc. recorded the following figures for the first six-month period last year:

	Feb Aug	Mar Sep	Apr Oct	May Nov	Jun Dec	Jul Jan
Sales						
Last Year	$8,000.00	14,000.00	16,000.00	13,000.00	10,000.00	9,000.00
Planned						

They are hoping for a 10% increase in sales during the coming period. Forecast the planned sales for the coming July.

Solution   *Step 1* Write the equation for monthly sales percentage.

$$Monthly\% = \left(\frac{Monthly\ \$Sales}{Last\ Year's\ Total\ \$Sales\ for\ Period} \right) 100\%$$

Step 2 Substitute $\left(\dfrac{Monthly\ \$Sales}{Last\ Year's\ \$Sales} \right)$ for the Monthly % in equation 5.1.

$$Pl.\ Sales = \left(\frac{Mon.\ \$Sales}{LY\ Total\ \$Sales} \right) \left(\frac{100\% + \$Sales\ Var.\%}{100\%} \right) LY\ Total\ \$Sales$$

$$= Monthly\ \$Sales \left(\frac{100\% + \$Sales\ Var.\%}{100\%} \right)$$

$$= \$9,000.00 \left(\frac{100\% + 10\%}{100\%} \right)$$

$$= \$9,000.00\ (1.10)$$

$$= \$9,900.00$$

Planning Sales for Different Number of Selling Days

As mentioned previously, the number of selling days in a given month can affect the sales plan. All else being equal, fewer selling days can cause an overestimation of sales, while more selling days would cause an underestimation of sales, especially for months that have high sales volume. Such holidays as Christmas, New Year's Day, Labor Day, and Thanksgiving deserve special consideration because the planned sales figures must reflect the number of selling days. This is calculated by multiplying the planned sales by the proportion of planned selling days to the number of selling days last year. The monthly planned sales figure (see *equation 5.1*) is modified slightly by including the number of planned selling days divided by the number of selling days last year. This ratio is used as multiplier in the formula. This concept is illustrated in equation 5.2:

EQUATION 5.2

$$\textbf{\textit{Mon. Pl. Sales}} =$$

$$\left(\frac{\textit{\#Pl. Days}}{\textit{\#Days LY}}\right)\left(\frac{\textit{Mon.\%}}{100\%}\right)\left(\frac{100\% + \textit{\$Sales Var.\%}}{100\%}\right)(\textit{LY Total \$Sales})$$

Problem   Recalculate Webster, Inc.'s planned sales for July using the fact that the coming July has 27 selling days as opposed to the 26 from the previous July. They were aiming for a 10% increase in sales and found that last year's total sales for the six-month period were $70,000, while the monthly percentage was 12.86%.

Solution

$$\textit{July Pl. Sales} =$$

$$\left(\frac{\textit{\#Pl. Days}}{\textit{\#Days LY}}\right)\left(\frac{\textit{Mon.\%}}{100\%}\right)\left(\frac{100\% + \textit{\$Sales Var.\%}}{100\%}\right)(\textit{LY Total \$Sales})$$

$$= \left(\frac{27}{26}\right)\left(\frac{12.86\%}{100\%}\right)\left(\frac{100\% + 10\%}{100\%}\right)(\$70,000.00)$$

$$= 1.0385\,(.1286)\,(1.10)\,(\$70,000.00)$$

$$= 1.0385\,(\$9,902.20)$$

$$= \$10,283.43$$

The planned sales are larger due to the extra selling day this year. If the number of selling days are less than last year, the planned sales figure will be less.

Problem   As a buyer for the Tiny Toys Store, Candy Williams noticed that the previous December contained 27 selling days, 21 before Christmas and 6 afterward. In the coming year there will be only 20 days before Christmas and 5 afterward. Candy is planning a 20% increase over last year's sales for the period of $165,000. From her "Beat Last Year" book she found that the sales before Christmas totaled $157,500 while those afterward totaled $6,600. Candy is considering making up for the two lost selling days by opening the store on Sunday for the two weeks before Christmas. To make this decision, she wants to find out how much difference the two days would make in her sales plan.

Solution   *Step 1* Write the equation for the monthly sales percentage before Christmas.

$$Pre\text{-}Xmas\ Mon.\% = \left(\frac{Pre\text{-}Xmas\ Mon.\ \$Sales}{LY\ Tot.\ \$Sales}\right)(100\%)$$

Step 2 Using the monthly sales formula (see *equation 5.1*), substitute $\frac{Pre\text{-}Xmas\ Mon.\ \$Sales}{LY\ Tot.\ \$Sales}$ for the pre-Christmas monthly percentage. Notice last year's total sales cancels out pre-Christmas planned sales:

$$Pre\text{-}Xmas\ Mon.\ \$Sales\left(\frac{100\% + \$Sales\ Var.\%}{100\%}\right)$$

Step 3 Find the pre-Christmas planned sales for 20 shopping days.

$$Pre\text{-}Xmas\ Pl.\ Sales(20) =$$

$$\left(\frac{\#Pl.\ Days}{\#Days\ LY}\right)(Pre\text{-}Xmas\ Mon.\$Sales)\left(\frac{100\% + \$Sales\ Var.\%}{100\%}\right)$$

$$= \left(\frac{20}{21}\right)(\$157,500.00)\left(\frac{100\% + 20\%}{100\%}\right)$$

$$= .9524\,(\$157,500.00)\,(1.20)$$

$$= .9524\,(\$189,000.00)$$

$$= \$180,003.60$$

Step 4 Find the pre-Christmas planned sales for 22 selling days. That is, if the store remains open the two Sundays before Christmas.

$$Pre\text{-}Xmas\ Pl.\ Sales(22) =$$

$$\left(\frac{\#Pl.\ Days}{\#Days\ LY}\right)(Pre\text{-}Xmas\ Mon.\ \$Sales)\left(\frac{100\% + \$Sales\ Var.\%}{100\%}\right)$$

$$= \left(\frac{22}{21}\right)(\$157,500.00)\left(\frac{100\% + 20\%}{100\%}\right)$$

$$= 1.0476\,(\$157,500.00)\,(1.20)$$

$$= 1.0476\,(\$189,000.00)$$

$$= \$197,996.40$$

Step 5 Find the difference in the pre-Christmas planned sales between 22 and 20 selling days.

$$Diff.\ in\ Pl.\ Sales = Pre\text{-}Xmas\ Pl.\ Sales(22) - Pre\text{-}Xmas\ Pl.\ Sales(20)$$

$$= \$197,996.40 - \$180,003.60$$

$$= \$17,992.80$$

Planning Sales for the Easter Holiday

In many areas of retailing, the Easter period provides a consumer spending stimulus as it signifies the beginning of spring. Planning for this holiday is different from others as it can fall anywhere from mid-March to mid-April. While buying new apparel for Easter Sunday is not as strong a concept as it used to be, consumers are still eager to purchase new items in the spring. Additionally, business is usually better when Easter falls late in April because people seem to be more prepared psychologically to purchase goods when surrounded by the warmer spring breezes of April, as opposed to the cold winds of a lingering winter in March.

Consequently, the two months of March and April often are planned together in such a way as to account for the varying date of Easter. Because the amount of business is a function not only of the number of selling days, but also the time of year, the basic monthly planned sales equation must be modified to reflect the proportion of the two-month total allotted each month. This calculation is demonstrated as follows:

EQUATION 5.3

$$\textbf{\textit{Monthly Planned Sales}} =$$

$$\frac{\textit{Last Mon.\%}}{\textit{Last Mar\%} + \textit{Last Apr\%}} \left(\frac{\textit{Last Mar\%} + \textit{Last Apr\%}}{100\%} \right) \left(\frac{100\% + \$\textit{Sales Var.\%}}{100\%} \right) \textit{LY \$Sales/Period}$$

Problem Clare McPhee is forecasting a 15% increase in sales for the first six-month period of next year. Easter will be on April 10th. The last time the holiday fell on that date, 16% of the sales were accounted for in March and 32% in April. Last year's figures show that of the $350,000 in sales, 10% occurred in March and 25% in April. What should be the planned sales for April?

Solution $\textit{April Pl. Sales} =$

$$\left(\frac{\textit{Last Apr\%}}{\textit{Last Mar\%} + \textit{Last Apr\%}} \right) \left(\frac{\textit{Mar\%} + \textit{Apr\%}}{100\%} \right) \left(\frac{100\% + \$\textit{Sales Var.\%}}{100\%} \right) (\textit{LY Tot. \$Sales/Period})$$

$$= \left(\frac{32\%}{16\% + 32\%} \right) \left(\frac{10\% + 25\%}{100\%} \right) \left(\frac{100\% + 15\%}{100\%} \right) (\$350,000.00)$$

$$= \left(\frac{32\%}{48\%} \right) \left(\frac{35\%}{100\%} \right) \left(\frac{115\%}{100\%} \right) (\$350,000.00)$$

$$= \left(\frac{.32}{.48} \right) (.35)(1.15)(\$350,000.00)$$

$$= \left(\frac{.32}{.48} \right) (.35)(\$402,500.00)$$

$$= \left(\frac{.32}{.48} \right) (\$140,875.00)$$

$$= \left(\frac{\$45,080.00}{.48} \right)$$

$$= \$93,916.67$$

Planning Sales with Fluctuating Prices

The retailer is always happy to see the dollar sales figure increase, especially in a stable market. But as prices climb the buyer cannot overlook the fact that growth may be due simply to inflation rather than an increase in the number of sales. With increasing prices, the number of transactions may decline causing the actual profit to decrease. In such situations, the monthly percentages may no longer be reliable indicators on which to plan sales. Instead a factor that estimates the change in the number of transactions is used. Fluctuations in the number of transactions per day or month should be anticipated. Seasonal buying habits are the most obvious reason for a rise or decline in the number of transactions. Pre-Christmas transactions are expected to be higher in most retail stores than pre-Fourth of July. The number of transactions should not be viewed alone but in conjunction with dollar sales figures. If sales are increasing but the number of transactions is relatively stable, consumers are purchasing more during each transaction or inflation has increased prices.

It is important to be aware of the pressures, issues, and events that may affect spending patterns and habits of the consumer. The number of transactions—as well as total sales—easily are affected by psychological, sociological, and economic occurrences. The ban on Tris-treated children's sleepwear caused many families simply to avoid purchasing sleepwear because Tris was thought to be carcinogenic (i.e., cancer-causing agent). A social change, such as interest in sports, health and fitness, caused the active sportswear (activewear) business to grow. When money is tight, as in times of inflation and recession, people alter spending habits and change priorities. Changes in competition also can cause the number and the size of transactions to fluctuate.

On any given day or a period, the number of transactions should be obtained in a simple manner. Any system that requires too much time and/or effort may not be worth the investment. In small retail stores, numbered sales slips usually serve the purpose. For example, if sales ticket number 09903 was the first in the sales book in the morning and at the end of the day number 09955 was the last ticket, simply subtract the beginning number from the ending number. In this case, there have been 52 transactions (provided there were no voided numbers or credits). If two sales receipts had been voided and three credits were issued, then there would have been 47 transactions (that is, subtract 5 from 52). Companies utilizing computer technology will receive not only a printout of the number of transactions, but also may be provided with an hourly recording. This hourly information is very useful in predicting personnel needs at various times of the day.

The number of transactions also may be used to plan sales. The underlying theory is that the planned sales equals the planned average sales multiplied by the planned total number of transactions for the period, as shown in the following:

Planned Sales = (Planned # Transactions)(Planned Average $Sales)

Next, write each factor in terms of known information, such as the actual number of transactions during the same period last year. The planned number of transactions is the percentage variation in transactions multiplied by the number of sales for the period last year, as illustrated:

$$Planned\ \#Transactions = \left(\frac{100\% + Transaction\ Var.\%}{100\%} \right)(\#Transactions)$$

Therefore substituting for the planned number of transactions in the planned sales equation gives:

$$Pl.\ Sales = \left(\frac{100\% + Trans.\ Var.\%}{100\%}\right)(\#Trans.)(Pl.\ Average\ \$Sales)$$

The planned average sales is the percentage variation in sales times the average sales, which may be written as last year's total sales for the period divided by the total number of transactions, as in:

$$Pl.\ Aver.\ Sales = \left(\frac{100\% + \$Sales\ Var.\%}{100\%}\right)\left(\frac{LY\ Sales/Period}{LY\#Trans.}\right)$$

Substituting for planned average sales in the planned sales equation gives the following result:

$$Pl.\ Sales = \left(\frac{100\% + Trans.\ Var.\%}{100\%}\right)(\#Trans.)\left(\frac{100\% + \$Sales\ Var.\%}{100\%}\right)\left(\frac{LY\$Sales/Per.}{\#Trans.}\right)$$

Thus, the number of transactions cancels out leaving equation 5.4:

EQUATION 5.4

$$Pl.\ Sales = \left(\frac{100\% + Trans.\ Var.\%}{100\%}\right)\left(\frac{100\% + \$Sales\ Var.\%}{100\%}\right)(LY\ Sales/Per.)$$

It is important to distinguish between the two types of variation. When talking about sales it is customary to use dollar amounts. The dollar sales variation ($Sales Variation) is always the change in the **dollar** amount of sales. Whereas, the change in **number** of sales is called the transaction variation. For this text, please refer to these terms as $Variation ($Var.) and #Variation (#Var.) respectively.

The transaction factor may be obtained by estimating the percentage variation in transactions. This estimate is based on prior experience and the percentage is entered into the formula directly. Alternatively, the percentage may be based on estimates of the actual number of sales. Suppose there were 400 items sold last year. Because the price for this item has increased you expect to sell only 360 items for the same period this year. The transaction variation percentage would be:

$$Tran.\ Var.\% =$$
$$\left(\frac{New - Old}{Old}\right)(100\%) = \left(\frac{360 - 400}{400}\right)(100\%) = \left(\frac{-40}{400}\right)(100\%) = -10\%$$

This 10% decrease is the transaction variation percentage you would use in *equation 5.4.*

No matter what equation is used to determine planned sales, it is still necessary to account for varying numbers of selling days and the changing holiday periods. The process is similar to that discussed previously (see *equations 5.2* and *5.3*); however, the monthly percentage figure is replaced by the change in the transaction factor. This is illustrated in the following problems.

Problem   As the price of lumber soars, so does the price of home furnishings. Jim Casey is the buyer for GoodKnights Furniture Store. Over the next six months he expects his costs to increase 20%, which in turn, he estimates, would cause the number of sales to decrease by 6%. Last year's sales for the same period amounted to $575,000. Estimate the planned sales for the period.

Solution

$$Pl.\ Sales =$$

$$\left(\frac{100\% + Trans.\ Var.\%}{100\%}\right)\left(\frac{100\% + \$Sales\ Var.\%}{100\%}\right)(LY\ \$Sales/Per.)$$

$$= \left(\frac{100\% - 6\%}{100\%}\right)\left(\frac{100\% + 20\%}{100\%}\right)(\$575,000.00)$$

$$= (.94)(1.20)(\$575,000.00)$$

$$= .94\ (\$690,000.00)$$

$$= \$648,600.00$$

Problem   The buyer for Haskell's Shoe Store is excited because the import duty on shoes has been lowered and shoes can now sell for 25% less than last year. This reduction should increase the number of transactions by 55%. Last September there were 25 selling days that brought in $11,800 in sales. Find the planned sales if September has only 24 selling days this year.

Solution

$$Mon.\ Pl.\ Sales =$$

$$\left(\frac{\#Pl.\ Days}{\#Days\ LY}\right)\left(\frac{100\% + Tran.Var.\%}{100\%}\right)\left(\frac{100\% + \$Sales\ Var.\%}{100\%}\right)(LY\ \$Sales/Sept.)$$

$$= \left(\frac{24}{25}\right)\left(\frac{100\% + 55\%}{100\%}\right)\left(\frac{100\% - 25\%}{100\%}\right)(\$11,800.00)$$

$$= .96\,(1.55)\,(.75)\,(\$11,800.00)$$

$$= 1.488\,(\$8,850.00)$$

$$= \$13,168.80$$

Problem   During the late fifties, sales of Easter bonnets declined steadily as hats went out of fashion. However, prices continued to climb due to the increased cost of labor and materials. The trade journals projected an 18% increase in prices. Janice Meekin, the buyer for Fiensteen's hat department during that period, estimated that the number of hats sold for Easter would be 250 as opposed to 1,100 for the year before. Janice knew that Easter would be early, April 2. Searching the records, she found that the last time that happened, March accounted for 10% of total sales and April accounted for 15%. If the sales for the previous March and April were $33,000, what were the planned sales for March using this planning method?

Solution   *Step 1* Find the transaction variation percentage.

$$Transaction\ Variation\% = \left(\frac{New - Old}{Old}\right)(100\%)$$

$$= \left(\frac{250 - 1100}{1100}\right)(100\%)$$

$$= \left(\frac{-850}{1100}\right)(100\%)$$

$$= -.7727(100\%)$$

$$= -77.27\%$$

Step 2 Find the planned sales for March.

$$Mar.\ Pl.\ Sales =$$

$$\left(\frac{Old\ Mar\%}{Old\ Mar\% + Old\ Apr\%}\right)\left(\frac{100\% + Tran\ Var.\%}{100\%}\right)\left(\frac{100\% + \$Sales\ Var.\%}{100\%}\right)(LY\ Sales\ Mar/Apr)$$

$$= \left(\frac{10\%}{10\% + 15\%}\right)\left(\frac{100\% - 77.27\%}{100\%}\right)\left(\frac{100\% + 18\%}{100\%}\right)(\$33,000.00)$$

$$= \left(\frac{.10}{.25}\right)(.2273)(1.18)(\$33,000.00)$$

$$= .40\,(.2273)(\$38,940.00)$$

$$= .40\,(\$8,851.06)$$

$$= \$3,540.42$$

Adjusting Planned Sales

As a period progresses, the actual sales are recorded on the sales plan. From this plan, the planned sales are compared to the actual sales to find the reliability of the predictions. When either the number of transactions or the level of sales fluctuates significantly, the planned sales figure should be adjusted, thereby controlling inventory.

What would cause differences between planned and actual sales? A sales plan is an estimate, and no one anticipates that the estimate will be equal to the achieved sales level. However, when sales differ greatly from projected levels, a number of factors may have contributed to the change. Higher sales figures might be caused by: 1) price inflation; 2) a competitor going out of business, thus providing a store with new customers; 3) the introduction of new customer services; 4) the introduction of new lines and/or the upgrading of a price line; or 5) an increase in promotion and advertising.

Lower sales figures might be caused by: 1) a decrease in disposable income; 2) competition taking sales away from the store; 3) a cutback in consumer services, advertising, or promotion; 4) the elimination of lines and/or price lines; or 5) a change in selling methods.

Adjusting the planned sales is a two-step procedure. First determine if the plan needs to be adjusted, by asking the question "What percentage of last year's sales equals this year's change in sales?"

$$Actual\ \$Sales\ Variation\ \% = \left(\frac{Actual\ \$Sales - Last\ Year\ \$Sales}{Last\ Year's\ \$Sales} \right)(100\%)$$

If the percentage differs greatly from the one that was used to estimate the planned sales, then the next step would be to adjust the planned sales. It is convenient to record the planned change percentage on the sales plan. To find the adjusted planned sales, apply one of the equations that was used for forecasting planned sales. The only difference is that the estimates for the percentage change are adjusted to reflect current conditions. The same reasoning also may be applied to changes in the number of transactions.

The original plan may have been made using an equation that employed monthly percentages and assumed stable prices. If prices begin to fluctuate, the adjusted sales should be planned using a different equation—one that employs the percentage variation in transactions.

In general, the percentage variation—be it in sales or transactions—is the difference between the new and the old divided by the old and multiplied by 100%. This resultant percentage is negative for decreases and positive for increases. The formula for this calculation is as follows:

EQUATION 5.5

$$Variation\% = \left(\frac{New - Old}{Old} \right) 100\%$$

Problem The sportswear buyer for Salak's Department Store finds that sales are running ahead of the plan. What is the actual variation percentage for the month of May?

$Sales	Feb	Mar	Apr	May	June	July
$Last Year	26,000	38,000	32,000	40,000	42,000	33,000
$Planned	28,600	418,000	352,000	44,000	46,200	36,300
$Actual	28,340	43,700	38,400	50,000		
Actual Var.%	9%	15%	20%			
$Adjusted						

Solution

$$Act.\ \$Var.\% = \left(\frac{New\ -\ Old}{Old}\right)100\%$$

$$= \left(\frac{\$50,000.00\ -\ \$40,000.00}{\$40,000.00}\right)100\%$$

$$= \left(\frac{\$10,000.00}{\$40,000.00}\right)100\%$$

$$= (.25)\,100\%$$

$$= 25\%$$

Problem The sportswear buyer for Salak's now must decide what action to take. The buyer reasons that the unusually hot weather has pushed swimwear and leisurewear sales to an all time high for the month of May. Weather predictions indicate that this climatic trend probably will continue throughout the rest of the spring season. Vendors can supply limited additions of merchandise through June 30th. By adjusting the planned sales, the buyer can determine whether or not an increase in merchandise is warranted. Find the adjusted sales for June and July.

Solution *Step 1* Find the adjusted planned sales for June.

$$June\ Adj.\ Sales = \left(\frac{100\%\ +\ Adj.\ \$Var.\%}{100\%}\right)LY's\ June\ \$Sales$$

$$= \left(\frac{100\%\ +\ 25\%}{100\%}\right)\$42,000.00$$

$$= (1.25)\,\$42,000.00$$

$$= \$52,500.00$$

Step 2 Find the adjusted planned sales for July.

$$July\ Adj.\ Sales = \left(\frac{100\%\ +\ Adj.\ \$Var.\%}{100\%}\right)LY's\ July\ \$Sales$$

$$= \left(\frac{100\%\ +\ 25\%}{100\%}\right)\$33,000.00$$

$$= (1.25)\,\$33,000.00$$

$$= \$41,250.00$$

These adjusted figures for June and July are each higher than their respective planned figures. Consequently, the buyer decides that the actual sales can increase if there is more merchandise on hand.

Problem The buyer responsible for holiday formal apparel notes that because of the poor economic conditions, sales are not up to their anticipated level. Examine the sales figures provided below and determine the actual percentage change for the month of November.

$Sales	Sept	Oct	Nov	Dec
$Last Year	14,000	22,000	39,000	47,000
$Planned	15,000	24,000	42,000	51,000
$Actual	14,000	21,500	37,000	
Actual Var.%	0	– 2%		
$Adjusted				

Solution

$$Actual\ \$Variation\% = \left(\frac{New - Old}{Old}\right)100\%$$

$$= \left(\frac{\$37,000.00 - \$39,000.00}{\$39,000.00}\right)100\%$$

$$= \left(\frac{-\$2,000.00}{\$39,000.00}\right)100\%$$

$$= -5.1282\%\ or\ -5.13\%$$

Problem The traffic in this same holiday formal department is low and the buyer feels this selling trend will continue. Adjust the sales for December accordingly.

Solution

$$Dec.\ Adj.\ \$Sales = \left(\frac{100\% + Adj.\ \$Var.\%}{100\%}\right)LY's\ Dec.\ \$Sales$$

$$= \left(\frac{100\% + (-5.13\%)}{100\%}\right)LY's\ Dec.\ \$Sales$$

$$= \left(\frac{100\% - 5.13\%}{100\%}\right)LY's\ Dec.\ \$Sales$$

$$= (.9487)\$47,000.00$$

$$= \$44,588.90$$

Adjusting Planned Sales Using Transactions

A number of factors may contribute to a required adjustment in planned sales. When planned sales figures are up and the number of transactions are also on the rise, you would be correct to assume that you are attracting more people who are purchasing more goods (or making repeat purchases), which in turn increases sales. If this is the case, chances are you will meet your planned sales goal.

However, if planned sales are increasing, but the number of transactions is down, it could mean that fewer people are buying merchandise and the apparent rise in sales could be due merely to inflation. In this instance, the buyer might be misled into thinking that the sales picture is stronger than it really is. On the other hand, if inflation is not as great as the increase in sales, the consumers who are purchasing are spending more per transaction.

When sales have decreased but the number of transactions has increased, more people are purchasing or making repeat purchases but at a lower dollar value per transaction. In this situation more suggestive selling might be used in to increase the total sales per transaction. Suggestive selling is a sales technique in which sales personnel offer additional suggestions as to what might be purchased to accompany an article selected by the consumer. For instance, when a customer is trying on a dress, the salesperson will select accessory items that would enhance the garment and increase the total sale.

If both sales and the number of transactions are decreasing, it is obvious that planned sales will not be attained (if they were intended to increase) and that people are not buying. In this instance, the retailer must analyze the situation and determine how to increase the sales and/or the number of transactions.

The equations needed for adjusting the planned sales while using both the percentage change in sales and transactions have been discussed. To find the percentage change in sales and the percentage of change in transactions use *equation 5.5*. The adjusted planned sales are calculated from *equation 5.4* and are illustrated in the following problem:

Problem   The Max Department Store china buyer has noted that planned sales for September were $12,000, which is $1,500 above last year's sales. Sales for the month of August were $13,500 or $2,000 above last year's figure. This situation seems to have resulted from the increased cost of the average item and/or an increase in the amount of each transaction and not because of an increase in the number of transactions. The number of transactions during August has declined by 10%. At this point, should the sales plan be adjusted? If so, by how much?

Solution   *Step 1* Find the percent sales variation of this year to last year for the month of August (see *equation 5.5*).

$$\$Sales\ Variation\% = \left(\frac{New - Old}{Old} \right) 100\%$$

$$= \left(\frac{\$2,000.00}{\$11,500.00} \right) 100\%$$

$$= 17.3913\%$$

Step 2 Find the adjusted planned sales for September (see *equation 5.4*).

$$Adj.\ Pl.\ Sales =$$

$$\left(\frac{100\% + Trans.\ Var.\%}{100\%} \right) \left(\frac{100\% + \$Sales\ Var.\%}{100\%} \right) LY's\ \$Sales$$

$$= \left(\frac{100\% - 10\%}{100\%} \right) \left(\frac{100\% + 17.39\%}{100\%} \right) \$10,500.00$$

$$= (.90)(1.1739)\$10,500.00$$

$$= (1.0565)\$10,500.00$$

$$= \$11,093.25$$

Step 3 Find the difference between adjusted and planned sales for September.

$$Amount\ of\ Adjustment = Adjusted - Planned$$
$$= \$11,093.25 - \$12,000.00$$
$$= -\$906.75$$

Because the adjusted planned sales for September is $906.75 less than planned, the sales plan should be reduced by this amount.

Computer Drill 20: Planning Sales

Planning Sales is the name of the computer program that generates six types of problems for this section of the text. The types of problems available are:

- *Planning Sales with Stable Prices*
- *Planning Sales for a Different Number of Selling Days*
- *Planning Sales for Easter Holiday*
- *Planning Sales with Fluctuating Prices*
- *Adjusting Planned Sales*
- *Adjusting Planned Sales using Transactions*

Assignments

1. The buyer for Woodward's expects a 13.0% increase in sales over last year's volume of $148,000.00. Last year 21.0% of the sales occurred in September. Project the planned sales for the coming September.

2. Swanson's manager notices that sales over the last few years have changed. Also prices have continued to rise because of the increased cost of labor and materials. Trade journals project a 25.0% increase in prices. The manager estimates that transactions will fall off 22.0%. Sales for the previous September, which had 22 selling days, were $22,000.00. What would be the planned sales figure for September this year, with 23 selling days?

3. The buyer for Davidson's noticed that the previous December contained 22 selling days before Christmas. In the coming year there will be 23 selling days before Christmas. Davidson's is planning an 8.0% increase over last year's sales for the period of $25,960.00. The pre-Christmas sales for last year totaled $22,000.00. What are the planned pre-Christmas sales for this December?

4. Swanson's expects a 9.0% increase in sales over last year's volume of $230,000.00. Last year, 20.0% of the sales occurred in May. Calculate the planned sales for May keeping in mind that this May has 22 selling days as opposed to 23 days the previous May.

5. Crompton's is forecasting a 13.0% increase in sales for the first six-month period of next year. Easter will fall on April 15th that year. The last time Easter fell on that date, 16.5% of the sales were accounted for in March and 17.0% in April. Last year's figures show that of $335,000.00 in sales, 24.0% occurred in March and April combined. What should the planned sales for April be?

PLANNING STOCK

After planning sales for a specific sales period, the next step in developing the six-month merchandising plan is determining stock levels. **Planned stock** must meet anticipated sales and yet be trim enough to avoid tying up excess capital. In establishing a stock plan, consideration should be given to such factors as basic stock, fashion items, special promotions, price lines, colors, and sizes. First it is important to decide how much stock is needed.

Methods for planning stock vary, but any method should consider: 1) merchandise needed for the opening of the period such as beginning-of-the-month stock; 2) what will be purchased during the period, i.e., planned purchases; and 3) the amount of stock on hand at the end of the period.

Four methods of planning stock are presented here. They are: 1) basic stock method or average plus variation; 2) percentage variation method; 3) stock-sales ratio method; and 4) week's supply method. All are based on retail figures because that is the most popular basis for these calculations. The first two stock planning methods are based on the difference between the planned sales and last year's sales. The last two methods are based on the ratio of planned sales to last year's sales. The last year's figure could be a figure for the entire year or one that represents a specific portion of the year. When calculating planned stock, be sure all figures in the formula represent the same period of time.

Basic Stock Method or Average Plus Variation

It is important to keep in mind that stock and sales do not always vary proportionally. As sales increase, average stock may decrease if not replenished. The end result is a higher turnover figure as sales are divided by a smaller, average stock number. Moreover, it may be important to retain a minimum level of some lines, sizes, or colors of items that sell well and are in constant demand.

In the **basic stock method or average plus variation**, the planned stock for the beginning of a period—usually a month—is written as the basic stock figure plus the planned sales for the period. The average stock is always going to be at least as high as last year's sales. Therefore, neither the basic stock figure or the planned stock ever will be negative. Using this method, the retailer has a larger investment in inventory because of the extra merchandise carried that increases inventory costs. Retailers with low turnover might use this method. The basic stock figure reflects the minimum level of stock that is to be maintained regardless of sales volume. Additionally, it is designed to meet sales and avoid out-of-stock conditions. This figure is determined by subtracting last year's sales for the period from the average stock. Calculation of the average stock is discussed in *Chapter Four, page 125.*

Planned Stock = (Average Stock − Last Year's $Sales) + Planned $Sales

Another way of looking at this method is to consider the planned stock to be equal to the average stock plus the variation or change in total dollar sales volume for the period. This is the reason this method sometimes is called average plus variation. The change or variation in sales is a quantity we used as a percentage in the section on planning sales and may be rewritten in terms of dollar sales as the difference between the planned sales and last year's sales. The planned stock is equal to the average stock plus the variation, i.e. the difference between planned dollar sales and last year's dollar sales. When planned sales minus last year's sales equals a negative number, this number is subtracted from average stock, due to the mathematics of the calculation. This formula is illustrated as follows:

EQUATION 5.6

Planned Stock = *Average Stock* + (*Planned $Sales* − *Last Year's $Sales*)

Problem   Last year, the Diablo men's wear department recorded sales of $5,500 for the month of October. They also recorded a BOM inventory of $2,300 for October and a BOM for November of $3,800. This year the planned sales for October are $6,700. What should the stock level be for the beginning of October?

Solution   *Step 1* Find the average stock (see *equation 4.7*).

$$Average\ Stock = (Beginning + End) \div \#Terms\ in\ Sum$$

$$= (\$2,300.00 + \$3,800.00) \div 2$$

$$= \$6,100.00 \div 2$$

$$= \$3,050.00$$

Step 2 Find the planned stock (see *equation 5.6*).

$$Planned\ Stock = Average\ Stock + (Planned\ \$Sales - LY's\ \$Sales)$$

$$= \$3,050.00 + \$6,700.00 - \$5,500.00$$

$$= \$4,250.00$$

Percentage Variation Method

Instead of adding 100% of the change or variation between planned sales and last year's sales directly to the average stock, as was done in the basic stock method, for the **percentage variation planned stock method**, one half the variation percentage multiplied by the average stock is added. This is the same variation (change) percentage as was computed in *equation 5.5*.

$$Planned\ Stock = Average\ Stock + \tfrac{1}{2}(Variation\%)Average\ Stock$$

Combining the average stock terms gives equation 5.7, as shown in the following:

EQUATION 5.7

$$Planned\ Stock = \left(\frac{100\% + \tfrac{1}{2}Variation\%}{100\%} \right)Average\ Stock$$

FIGURE 5.3

Relationship Between Turnover and Percentage of Variation Added to Average Stock

Average Period Between Reorders	Turnover/Year	Percentage
2 years	0	0.00
1 year	$\frac{1}{2}$	100.00
6 months	1	50.00
4 months	2	25.00
3 months	3	16.66
	4	12.50
	5	10.00
2 months	6	8.33
	7	7.14
	8	6.25
	9	5.55
	10	5.00
	11	4.54
1 month	12	4.16

This is the easiest stock planning formula to use, as the formula is simple and the information is easy to obtain. However, to see the relationship of this method to the basic stock method consider the formula prior to equation 5.7:

$$Planned\ Stock = Aver.\ Stock + \tfrac{1}{2}\ Variation\%\,(Aver.\ Stock)$$

which is rewritten as:

$$Planned\ Stock = Aver.\ Stock + \tfrac{1}{2}\ Aver.\ Stock\left(\frac{Planned\ Sales - LY\$Sales}{LY\$Sales}\right)100\%$$

Because stock turnover equals sales divided by average stock, we can make the following substitution:

$$Planned\ Stock = Aver.\ Stock + \frac{1}{2(Turnover)}\,(Planned\ Sales - LY\$Sales)$$

Figure 5.3 shows how the percent variation or difference between planned and last year's sales—which is added to the average stock—varies with the stock turnover. The percentage variation and basic stock methods are identical when the variation or difference is 0 or the turnover is $\frac{1}{2}$ and both are unprofitable situations.

Most texts indicate the basic stock method is adequate when the turnover is under six times per year while the percentage variation method is superior for a turnover of six or more. In the latter instance, the average period between reorders is two months or less, making it less a necessity to cushion the projected sales figures when the turnover rate is low and the period between reorders is greater. A higher stock level is derived under the basic stock method to provide for an unforeseen increase in sales that could not be covered spontaneously.

Problem In the previous problem, calculating the stock level for the Diablo men's wear department, we found the average stock to be $3,050, while the planned sales were $6,700, and last year's sales for the period were $5,500. For this calculation, use the percentage variation method to find the planned stock level.

Solution *Step 1* Find the sales variation percentage.

$$Variation\% = (\frac{Planned - LY}{LY}) \, 100\%$$

$$= \left(\frac{\$6,700.00 - \$5,500.00}{\$5,500.00} \right) 100\%$$

$$= \left(\frac{\$1,200.00}{\$5,500.00} \right) 100\%$$

$$= 21.82\%$$

Step 2 Find the planned stock level (see *equation 5.7*).

$$Planned \, Stock = \left(\frac{100\% + \frac{1}{2} \, Variation\%}{100\%} \right) Average \, Stock$$

$$= \left(\frac{100\% + \frac{1}{2} \, (21.82\%)}{100\%} \right) \$3,050.00$$

$$= \left(\frac{100\% + 10.91\%}{100\%} \right) \$3,050.00$$

$$= \left(\frac{110.91\%}{100\%} \right) \$3,050.00$$

$$= \$3,382.76$$

Stock-Sales Ratio Method

Another method of planning stock is the **stock-sales ratio method**, which is found by multiplying the BOM stock-sales ratio by the planned sales for the period, as illustrated in the following formula:

EQUATION 5.8

BOM Planned Stock = (BOM Stock-Sales Ratio) Planned Sales

The planned stock equals the beginning of the month stock-sales ratio multiplied by the planned sales for the month. Stock-sales ratios are published yearly (for previous years) by the National Retail Federation in *Retail Horizons: Benchmarks for [Year XXXX], Forecasts for [Year XXXX]*. The figures are shown for large department stores and specialty stores and are segmented by type of retail operation and sales volume. Similar information can be located on the U.S. Census Web site. These stock-sales ratios are presented by product type under North American Industry Classification System (NAICS), the product identification system. Timeliness of data can be an issue with government documents. Typically, the most recent data is two years old. It can serve as an effective alternative for general trends.

The BOM stock-sales ratio method is most appropriate when the stock and sales are expected to vary proportionately. The BOM stock, however, is generally higher than or equal to the average stock and no provisions are made in the formula to maintain a basic stock level. Therefore, in the planning stage, when sales are up, the projected stock level may be too high and when sales are down, the projected stock levels may be too low.

Problem Hanow's Elegant Furs maintains a stock-sales ratio of 2.2. The planned sales for November are $48,000.00. Find the planned stock level.

Solution

$$Planned\ Stock = (Stock\text{-}Sales\ Ratio)\ Planned\ Sales$$

$$= (2.2)\,\$48,000.00$$

$$= \$105,600.00$$

Problem Once again consider the Diablo's men's wear department. Remember that the average stock was $3,050.00, last year's sales for October were $5,500.00, and this year's planned sales for October are $6,700.00. Use the stock-sales ratio to find the planned stock level.

Solution

$$Planned\ Stock = \left(\frac{Average\ Stock}{Last\ Year's\ \$Sales}\right) Planned\ Sales$$

$$= \left(\frac{\$3,050.00}{\$5,500.00}\right) \$6,700.00$$

$$= (.5545)\,\$6,700.00$$

$$= \$3,715.15$$

Week's Supply Method

The **week's supply method** may be used for planning staple merchandise that has relatively little sales fluctuation. It is based, as the name implies, on weekly figures. The planned stock is determined by the number of week's supply multiplied by the average weekly planned sales.

$$Planned\ Stock = Number\ of\ Week's\ Supply\,(Weekly\ Planned\ Sales)$$

The number of week's supply equals the number of weeks in the period divided by the stock turnover for the same period. Therefore, the planned stock figure is calculated by dividing the number of week's supply by the stock turnover and multiplying by the weekly planned sales figure. This is demonstrated in the following equation:

EQUATION 5.9

$$Planned\ Stock\ =\ \left(\frac{Number\ of\ Weeks}{Stock\ Turnover}\right)Weekly\ Planned\ Sales$$

This method is similar to the stock-sales ratio in that stock and sales vary proportionately and both methods are based on the ratio of planned to previous sales. The relationship becomes more obvious if stock turnover is written in terms of sales and the factors are regrouped, as in:

$$Planned\ Stock\ =\ (\#Weeks)(Aver.\ Stock)\left(\frac{Weekly\ Planned\ Sales}{LY's\ Total\ \$Sales}\right)$$

Notice that the week's supply method uses the average stock instead of the beginning-of-the-month stock and the average weekly planned sales instead of planned sales for the period.

Problem Tiny's T-Shirt Shop has a stock turnover of 1.5 for the month. Weekly sales of $345.00 are planned in the next four weeks. Calculate the planned stock level using the week's supply method.

Solution
$$Planned\ Stock\ =\ \left(\frac{\#Weeks}{Stock\ Turnover}\right)Weekly\ Planned\ Sales$$

$$=\ \left(\frac{4}{1.5}\right)\$345.00$$

$$=\ \$920.00$$

Computer Drill 21: Planning Stock

Planning Stock is the name of the computer program that generates four types of problems for this section of the text. The types of problems available are:

- *Basic Stock Method or Average Plus Variation Method*
- *Percentage Variation Method*
- *Stock-Sales Ratio Method*
- *Week's Supply Method*

Assignments

1. Crompton's junior department has a stock turnover of 2.7. The planned sales for October are $8,949.60. Last year, Crompton's recorded a BOM inventory of $2,680.00 for October and a BOM inventory for November of $4,100.00. Last year's sales in the junior department totaled $6,780.00 for the month of October. Based on the stock turnover, calculate the planned stock for the beginning of October. (Choose between either the basic stock method or the percentage variation method.)

2. Hoffmann's candy department has a stock turnover of 4.0 for the month. Weekly sales of $1,860.00 are planned for the next four weeks. Calculate the planned stock level.

3. Last year, Hoffmann's Christmas department recorded sales of $5,660.00 for the month of November. They also recorded a BOM inventory of $1,460.00 for November, and a BOM for December of $4,200.00. This year the planned sales for November are $7,018.40. Using the basic stock method, calculate the planned stock level for the beginning of November.

4. The home furnishings department maintains a stock-sales ratio of 2.5. The planned sales for February are $8,073.60. Find the planned stock level.

PLANNING MARKUPS AND MARKDOWNS

In Chapter One, we discussed the concept of the initial markup. Remember that the initial markup is the difference between the first retail price placed on an article and the cost of the item. The initial markup must be large enough to cover operating expenses and reductions. It also must provide operating profit. In this chapter we are interested in planning the markups and markdowns. While some items carry a high initial markup percentage and some a low initial markup percentage, it is the overall initial markup that is estimated.

When deciding on an overall initial markup figure, we must be assured that it will provide ample revenue for such things as: 1) reductions, markdowns, discounts, and shortages; 2) **operating expenses**, which include selling expenses, management salaries, office supplies, rent, depreciation of fixtures, and uncollectible accounts; and 3) profit. A lack of revenue to cover the basic expenses will not provide enough income for profit. Thus, in planning an initial markup figure or percentage, all of the listed factors above must be taken into account.

The initial markup and sales projections must be planned with markdowns, discounts, and shortages in mind. These reductions are so inevitable that they are itemized on the merchandising plan. Discounts, shortages, operating expenses, and profit are listed as a percentage of planned sales for the period.

Using the Merchandising Plan to Estimate Markdowns

A growing percentage of markdowns may reflect a declining economic climate, poor selection of merchandise, or the shift of consumer attitude away from a specific classification of merchandise. Not all departments or stores will be uniform in the frequency or depth of markdowns. In women's fashion apparel, for instance, the markdowns are likely to be greater than in departments carrying a greater percentage of staple commodities. The seasonability of items within a department also will affect those markdown percentages in specific months. The markdown percentage is anticipated to be higher when sales are in progress or at the end of a season.

Markdowns are projected as a percentage of planned sales. A declining markdown percentage could indicate proficient buying to serve consumer needs and wants, or it could signify a hesitancy on the part of the buyer to reduce merchandise at an appropriate rate. In the markdown section of this book you learned that markdowns can be used to attract customers, to clear the floor of slow moving merchandise, or to consolidate price lines. When markdowns are being planned, such factors must be considered as possible contributors to a change in the number and depth of markdowns being taken.

The seven steps involved in using the merchandising plan to estimate markdowns are:

1. Record the actual markdowns taken last year as well as the dollar sales.
2. For each month, find last year's markdown as a percentage of last year's total sales.
3. For the period, find the last year's net markdown percentage.
4. Record the planned markdown percentages for this year.
5. Calculate the total planned dollar sales.

6. For each month, find the planned dollar markdown by multiplying the total planned sales by the monthly planned markdown percentage.

7. Find the planned net markdown percentage.

(Please note: the first three steps give you a basis for planning this year's markdowns. You may plan the markdowns to be comparable to last year or you may decide to adjust one or more of the monthly percentages.)

Problem   Last year's records for Greenfield's Department Store read as follows: (Steps 1 and 5)

$Sales	Feb Aug	Mar Sept	Apr Oct	May Nov	Jun Dec	July Jan	Total (Net)
Last Year$	35,000	32,000	33,000	37,000	45,000	36,000	218,000
Plan$	37,000	36,000	37,000	39,000	45,000	41,000	235,000
Actual$							
Variation%							
Adjusted Plan							
Markdowns							
Last year$	4,200	3,200	3,300	4,810	4,500	5,400	25,410
(%LYRT Sales)	1.93	1.47	1.51	2.21	2.06		
Planned$							
(%Plan Sales)							
Actual$							

Find the markdown percentage for last July (Step 2).

Solution   Use *equation 2.5.*

$$MD\% = \left(\frac{Last\ Year's\ \$MD\ July}{Last\ Year's\ Net\ \$Sales} \right) 100\%$$

$$= \left(\frac{\$5,400.00}{\$218,000.00} \right) 100\%$$

$$= (.02477)\ 100\%$$

$$= 2.48\%$$

Problem   Find the net markdown percentage for last year (step 3).

Solution

$$Net\ MD\% = \left(\frac{Net\ \$MD}{Net\ \$Sales} \right) 100\%$$

$$= \left(\frac{\$25,410.00}{\$218,000.00} \right) 100\%$$

$$= (.1166)\ 100\%$$

$$= 11.66\%$$

Problem   The owner of Greenfield's plans total sales of $235,000 and would like to keep the net markdown percentage about the same as last year.

The monthly planned percentages are similar to last year's (step 4). These planned percentages are used to calculate the planned dollar markdowns.

	Feb Aug	Mar Sept	Apr Oct	May Nov	Jun Dec	July Jan	Total (Net)
$Markdowns							
Planned$	4,465	3,525	3,525	5,170	4,700		
%Planned Sales	1.9	1.5	1.5	2.2	2.0	2.5	

Find the planned dollar markdown for July (step 6).

Solution

$$\$MD = \frac{Planned\ Net\ \$Sales \times Planned\ MD\%\ July}{100\%}$$

$$= \frac{\$235,000.00 \times 2.5\%}{100\%}$$

$$= \$235,000.00\,(.025)$$

$$= \$5,875.00$$

Problem What is the planned net markdown percentage for Greenfield's Department Store?

Solution *Step 1* Find the planned net dollar markdown (step 7).

$$Pl.\ Net\ \$MD = \$MD\ Feb + \$MD\ Mar + \$MD\ Apr$$
$$+ \$MD\ May + \$MD\ Jun + \$MD\ Jul$$

$$= \$4,465.00 + \$3,525.00 + \$3,525.00$$
$$+ \$5,170.00 + \$4,700.00 + \$5,875.00$$

$$= \$27,260.00$$

Step 2 Find the planned net markdown percentage (see *equation 2.11*).

$$Net\ MD\% = \left(\frac{Net\ \$MD}{Net\ \$Sales}\right) 100\%$$

$$= \left(\frac{\$27,260.00}{\$235,000.00}\right) 100\%$$

$$= (.116)\ 100\%$$

$$= 11.6\%$$

Using the Merchandising Plan to Estimate Initial Markups

After the planned net markdown percentage is calculated we turn our attention to the markup section of the merchandising plan. Last year's markup figures are helpful when planning this year's figures. The cumulative (actual) markup figures from last year's plan become the maintained (i.e, last year's) figures on the current plan. If no prior figures are available, this section on the plan would remain blank.

The initial (planned) markup reflects operating profits, operating expenses, markdowns, discounts, and shortages. These figures are recorded as percentages on the merchandising plan. It is a simple matter to use *equation 1.18* to calculate the initial markup percentage. It is customary to use the same initial markup percentage for each month in the planning period.

Problem A portion of the six-month merchandising plan for John's Salon is as follows:

Gross Margin	$121,800	Cash Discount	4%
Operating Expenses	$ 98,600	Allowable MD	10%
Operating Profit	$ 23,200	Shortage	6%
		Discount	5%
		Season Turnover	6

$Sales	Feb Aug	Mar Sept	Apr Oct	May Nov	Jun Dec	July Jan	Total (Net)
Last Year	50,000	65,000	78,000	95,000	112,000	100,000	500,000
Plan	60,000	76,000	90,000	108,000	126,000	120,000	580,000
Actual$							
Variation%							
Markup							
Maint.%(LY)	32%	33%	37%	39%	40%	36%	36%
Planned Initial%							
Actual Cum.%							

Find the initial markup for the period.

Solution **Step 1** Find the reduction percentage.

$$Red.\% = MD\% + Disc.\% + Shortage\%$$

$$= 10\% + 5\% + 6\%$$

$$= 21\%$$

Step 2 Find the operating expense as a percentage of the total planned dollar sales.

$$Operating\ Expense\% = \left(\frac{Operating\ Expense\$}{Planned\ \$Sales} \right) 100\%$$

$$= \left(\frac{\$98,600.00}{\$580,000.00} \right) 100\%$$

$$= (17)\ 100\%$$

$$= .17$$

Step 3 Find the operating profit as a percentage of the total planned dollar sales.

$$Operating\ Profit\% = \left(\frac{Operating\ Profit\$}{Planned\ \$Sales} \right) 100\%$$

$$= \left(\frac{\$23,200.00}{\$580,000.00} \right) 100\%$$

$$= (.04)\ 100\%$$

$$= 4\%$$

Step 4 Find the initial markup percentage for the period (see equation 1.18).

$$Init.\ MU\% = \left(\frac{Oper.\ Exp.\% + Oper.\ Profit\% + Red.\%}{100\% + Red.\%} \right) 100\%$$

$$= \left(\frac{17\% + 4\% + 21\%}{100\% + 21\%} \right) 100\%$$

$$= \left(\frac{42\%}{121\%} \right) 100\%$$

$$= (.3471)\ 100\%$$

$$= 34.7\%$$

Using the Merchandising Plan to Calculate Actual Markups

To calculate the actual markup for a given month, purchases must be maintained at cost. The actual dollar markup is the difference between the actual cost and the actual selling price of the merchandise in the specified period. The actual dollar markup is in fact the cumulative dollar markup for the unit of time under consideration. Cumulative dollar markup is described in *equation 1.7*. Similarly, the actual markup percentage for a specified unit of time is the average markup percentage described in *equation 1.8*.

Problem Keefer's Record Shop produced the following six-month sales plan:

$Sales	Feb Aug	Mar Sept	Apr Oct	May Nov	Jun Dec	July Jan	Total (Net)
Last Year$	8,000	7,500	8,500	9,000	10,500	8,500	52,000
Planned$	8,300	7,800	8,900	9,500	11,500	9,000	55,000
Actual$	8,260	7,900	8,800	9,900	10,700	8,440	54,000
Adjusted Plan							
Purchases (Cost)							
Last year$	4,800	4,500	5,200	5,400	6,300	5,000	31,200
Planned$	4,700	4,700	5,500	5,700	6,200	5,200	32,000
Actual$	4,770	4,800	5,550	5,800	6,350	5,230	32,500
Adjusted Plan							
Markup							
Maint.LY$	3,200	3,000	3,300	3,600	4,200	3,500	20,800
%							
Planned$ Initial	3,600	3,100	3,400	3,800	5,300	3,800	23,000
%							
Actual Cum.$							
%							

What are the actual dollar markup and the actual markup percentage for February?

Solution **Step 1** Find the cumulative dollar markup (see *equation 1.7*).

$$Cumulative\ \$MU = \$Retail - \$Cost$$

$$= \$8,260.00 - \$4,770.00$$

$$= \$3,490.00$$

Step 2 Find the average markup percentage (see *equation 1.8*).

$$MU\% = \left(\frac{Cumulative\ \$MU}{\$Retail}\right)100\%$$

$$= \left(\frac{\$3,490.00}{\$8,260.00}\right)100\%$$

$$= (.4225)\ 100\%$$

$$= 42.25\%$$

Problem Using the same six-month plan, what is the actual markup percentage for the period?

Solution **Step 1** Find the actual dollar markup for the period (see *equation 1.7*).

$$Total\ Cumulative\ \$MU = Total\ \$Retail - Total\ \$Cost$$

$$= \$54,000.00 - \$32,500.00$$

$$= \$21,500.00$$

Step 2 Find the actual markup percentage for the period (see *equation 1.8*).

$$AMU\%\ for\ period = \left(\frac{Total\ Cumulative\ \$MU}{Total\ \$Retail}\right)100\%$$

$$= \left(\frac{\$21,500.00}{\$54,000.00}\right)100\%$$

$$= 39.81\%$$

Computer Drill 22: Planning Markups and Markdowns

Planning Markups and Markdowns is the name of the computer program that generates three types of problems for this section of the text. The types of problems available are:

- *Using the Merchandising Plan to Estimate Markdowns*
- *Using the Merchandising Plan to Estimate Initial Markups*
- *Using the Merchandising to Calculate Actual Markups*

Assignments

1. Below are last year's figures for a music store:

$Sales	Feb Aug	Mar Sept	Apr Oct	May Nov	June Dec	July Jan	Total
Last Year$	40,000.00	37,000.00	41,000.00	46,000.00	53,000.00	47,000.00	264,000.00
Planned$	46,000.00	39,000.00	44,000.00	48,000.00	59,000.00	50,000.00	286,000.00
Markdowns							
Last Year$	4,300.00	3,800.00	4,200.00	5,100.00	4,900.00	5,790.00	28,090.00
%LY RT Sales	1.63	1.44	1.59	1.93	1.86	2.19	
Planned$	4,290.00	4,004.00	4,576.00				
%Planned Sales	1.50	1.40	1.60	1.90	2.20		

What was the net markdown percentage for last year?

2. The music store owner would like to keep the net markdown percentage about the same as last year's. With planned sales of $286,000.00, what would be the planned dollar markdown for November?

3. Determine the music store's planned dollar markdown for December.

4. The music store produced the following six-month sales plan:

$Sales	Feb Aug	Mar Sept	Apr Oct	May Nov	June Dec	July Jan	Total
Last Year$	7,600.00	7,100.00	8,000.00	8,600.00	9,600.00	8,400.00	49,300.00
Planned$	8,000.00	7,500.00	8,600.00	9,000.00	10,000.00	9,000.00	52,100.00
Actual$	7,400.00	6,800.00	7,900.00	8,100.00	10,300.00	9,900.00	50,400.00
$Purchases							
Last Year$	5,000.00	4,700.00	5,300.00	5,600.00	6,000.00	5,400.00	32,000.00
Planned$	5,600.00	4,300.00	5,000.00	5,200.00	6,500.00	5,100.00	31,700.00
Actual$	4,657.00	4,624.00	4,977.00	5,346.00	7,107.00	6,039.00	32,760.00
$Markups							
Maintained LY	$3,200.00	$3,000.00	$3,500.00	$3,900.00	$4,400.00	$3,800.00	21,800.00
Initial$	3,400.00	3,400.00	4,000.00	4,200.00	4,900.00	4,300.00	24,200.00

Find the actual dollar markup for March.

5. Find the music store's actual markup percentage for May.

6. What is the music store's actual markup percentage for the period?

7. Part of the six-month merchandising plan for Newkirk's Designer Furnishings is as follows:

Gross Margin	$159,300.00	Allowable MD	16.0%
Operating Expenses	$116,820.00	Shortage	5.0%
Operating Profit	$ 42,480.00	Discount	4.0%
Cash Discount	3.0%	Season Turnover	6

$Sales	Feb / Aug	Mar / Sept	Apr / Oct	May / Nov	June / Dec	July / Jan	Total
Last Year$	48,000.00	56,000.00	69,000.00	84,000.00	99,000.00	89,000.00	445,000.00
Planned$	64,000.00	67,000.00	87,000.00	96,000.00	112,000.00	105,000.00	531,000.00
Markup							
Maintained.% (LY)	29.0	32.0	35.0	39.0	42.0	38.0	

What is Newkirk's reduction percentage?

PLANNING PURCHASES

We are now ready to use the merchandising budget to plan purchases. The **planned purchases** figure represents the dollar amount of merchandise that will maintain the balance between stock and sales. Purchases can be planned for an entire store, a department, a classification, or a line. Because most stores use the retail method, purchases usually are planned at retail.

Planning Purchases at Retail

The planned purchases figure is the dollar amount to be brought into stock minus the dollar amount of stock already on hand, as shown in this simple formula:

$$Planned\ Purchases = \$Stock\ Needed - \$Stock\ On\ Hand$$

The amount of stock to be brought in during a period should be the amount necessary to cover the planned sales plus the planned reductions plus the planned stock for the end of the period. If the period is a month, we would need the planned EOM stock figure. (Remember this figure is the same as the planned BOM for the following month.) The stock-on-hand is the planned BOM for the month in question. This is illustrated in the following equation:

EQUATION 5.10

$$Planned\ Purchases = Sales + Reductions + EOM\ Stock - BOM\ Stock$$

Problem Generally, the month of December is the highest sales period for most stores in the United States. In preparation for the holiday selling period, the manager of the Pret-A-Portee Specialty Stores plans an EOM stock of $300,000 for November 30. During the November selling period, sales are estimated at $90,000 and reductions at $10,500. If Pret-A-Portee's November BOM stock was $220,000, what should be the planned purchases figure for the month of November?

Solution

$$Pl.\ Purch. = Sales + Red. + EOM\ Stock - BOM\ Stock$$

$$= \$90,000.00 + \$10,500.00 + \$300,000.00 - \$220,000.00$$

$$= \$180,500.00$$

Problem Because they have many years experience, the owners of the Ski Shop recognize that June and July are the slowest selling periods for their establishment. In preparation for these slow-selling months, June will start with stock of $45,000. Sales for the month are anticipated to be $12,000, markdowns $2,000, and shortages $500. The owners would like to begin the month of July with no more than $35,000 invested in retail stock. What should the planned purchases be for the month of July to maintain this inventory level?

Solution   *Step 1* Find dollar reductions.

$$\$Reduction = \$Markdown + \$Shortage$$

$$= \$2,000.00 + \$500.00$$

$$= \$2,500.00$$

Step 2 Find the planned prchases.

$$Pl.\ Purch. = Sales + Red. + EOM\ Stock - BOM\ Stock$$

$$= \$12,000.00 + \$2,500.00 + \$35,000.00 - \$45,000.00$$

$$= \$4,500.00$$

Planning Purchases at Cost

We have just calculated the retail dollars needed for purchases. Now the question is: "How much money do we need to pay for the goods?" To find the planned purchases at cost, use a modification of the dollar cost formula shown in Chapter One (see *equation 1.4*). This formula is:

$$\$Cost = \$Retail \left(\frac{Complement\ of\ RMU\%}{100\%} \right)$$

When calculating the planned purchases at cost, however, the dollar cost becomes purchases at cost, the dollar retail becomes purchases at retail, and the complement of the retail markup percentage is written as 100% minus the initial markup percentage. The resulting formula follows:

EQUATION 5.11

$$Purchases\ at\ Cost = Planned\ Purchases\ at\ Retail \left(\frac{100\% - Initial\ MU\%}{100\%} \right)$$

Problem   The owner of Goodie-Two Shoes Footwear is forecasting the business figures for the coming year. Included is a planned purchases figure of $250,000 and an initial markup percentage of 58%. If the owner adheres to these figures what will be the purchase cost?

Solution   Find purchases at cost.

$$Purch.\ at\ Cost = \$Pl.\ Purch.\ at\ Ret. \left(\frac{100\% - Init.\ MU\%}{100\%} \right)$$

$$= \$250,000.00 \left(\frac{100\% - 58\%}{100\%} \right)$$

$$= \$250,000.00 \left(\frac{42\%}{100\%} \right)$$

$$= \$250,000.00\,(.42)$$

$$= \$105,000.00$$

Computer Drill 23: Planning Purchases

Planning Purchases is the name of the computer program that generates two types of problems for this section of the text. The types of problems available are:

- *Planning Purchases at Retail*
- *Planning Purchases at Cost*

Assignments

1. The manager of Calddore plans an EOM stock of $310,000.00 for the end of May. During the May selling period, sales are estimated at $90,000.00, and reductions at $9,800.00. If Calddore's April EOM stock was $210,000.00, what would be the planned purchases for May?

2. In forecasting business figures for the coming year, Ling-Poi's owner is including planned purchases of $22,000.00, and an initial markup percentage of 53.0%. What is Ling-Poi's cost of purchases figure?

3. With sales up, Haldamne's planned sales volume for March is $64,000.00. Their manager plans reductions of $2,500.00. Haldamne has $190,000.00 stock-on-hand at the end of February. The manager plans an EOM stock of $310,000.00 for March. Find the planned purchases for March.

4. During the coming year, the Bugle plans purchases of $90,000.00, with an initial markup of 47.0% and a net markdown percentage of 8.0%. If management makes decisions based on these figures, what will be the cost of purchase figure?

5. The summer-selling period is a slow time of year for Snowmobile International. They will start the month of June with $340,000.00 stock-on-hand. Anticipated sales and reductions for June are $14,000.00 and $2,000.00 respectively. The owner would like to begin July with no more than $380,000.00 invested in retail stock. What should be the planned purchases for June to maintain this inventory level?

PLANNING OPEN-TO-BUY

Because experienced buyers attempt to distribute their orders over a period of time and because not all merchandise arrives exactly as scheduled, it is important to monitor how much money can be spent for new items. The term **open-to-buy (OTB)** refers to the amount of unspent money that is available for purchasing merchandise to be delivered during a given period. This figure represents the financial resources available to the buyer. It is the means of adding fresh merchandise to existing inventory. This calculation may be made for any time period, but is made usually for a month or a season. In larger operations, the calculations may be done weekly. To maintain effective control of the amount of merchandise available, open-to-buy should be adjusted as the buyer proceeds through a period.

There are several ways a buyer can increase the open-to-buy figure. The buyer can increase **planned markdowns** (an estimate of markdowns projected as a percentage of sales) or transfer outstanding orders to a later month. By increasing sales, the inventory is reduced and revenue can be reinvested in fresh stock. Increasing planned sales is a way to create OTB, but if the plan is not met there will be an excess stock level at the end of the period. Markdowns can produce the same effect because they are intended to stimulate sales, increase the need for new merchandise, and provide funds that can be reinvested. Some methods that are used by buyers are not equally ethical, such as reducing merchandise ordered by returning goods to vendors or canceling orders that are outstanding but not yet past the due date.

As mentioned, markdowns can be taken solely to increase the open-to-buy. However, taking too many markdowns that are not justified may reduce the possibility of attaining the maintained markup goal. Another way to increase the open-to-buy figure is to recalculate the status of on-order merchandise. If a delivery is past the due date, the order can be canceled because the contract has not been met by the vendor. In this case, the figure for on-order merchandise would be reduced. Yet another method is to ascertain if an order is outstanding but yet the due date has not been surpassed. The buyer should determine the likelihood of the arrival of this order within the month. Merchandise that will not arrive within the month may be put on next month's on-order list and removed from this month's figures. This also would increase the OTB.

In many instances, the merchandise manager is responsible for calculating the open-to-buy figure for the buyer. In other cases, the buyer calculates the open-to-buy and consults with the merchandise manager for approval of the plan. Regardless of which method is utilized, the ultimate purpose is to provide a working plan that will monitor spending. Some buyers think of the open-to-buy as their "checkbook"—which should be balanced always and seldom, if ever, overdrawn. As with other summary techniques, this plan is only as accurate as the projections utilized and often it is necessary to revise or adjust the plan. Unlike most checking accounts, an "overdrawn" open-to-buy may have no penalty if the plan has been revised and the merchandise manager has approved the additional spending. Spending in excess of the plan may be necessary particularly when prices on purchases are made available that have the potential to be lucrative for the operation. In another instance, merchandise might arrive earlier than anticipated, thus increasing inventory and reducing planned purchases. This could happen at a time when you have more immediate needs in other merchandise lines. Another reason for exceeding planned purchases would be to meet an unanticipated demand that has drained the stock supply before the plan could be revised.

BOM Open-to-Buy

The open-to-buy figure is the planned purchases minus merchandise received and merchandise already on order for the period. The on-order merchandise includes merchandise in transit and orders not yet shipped but due during the period. Open-to-buy can be calculated weekly, monthly, quarterly, or for any other realistic period.

Because the OTB is based on several figures in the sales and merchandising plan, it is figured first in terms of retail dollars. Consequently, if a dollar cost figure is desired, only the OTB figures need to be converted. The calculation to find OTB is illustrated in the following:

EQUATION 5.12

OTB = Planned Purchases − Merchandise Received − Merchandise On Order

---

Problem The KOTS Company's merchandising plan for October 1–31 has a planned beginning inventory of $44,000 and a closing inventory of $48,000. During this period, sales are estimated to be around $117,000, markdowns $2,000, and shortages $1,000. Currently the merchandise in stock is $100,000 and there are outstanding orders totaling $20,000. What is their OTB at retail?

Solution *Step 1* Find the total dollar reductions.

$$\$Reductions = \$Discounts + \$Markdowns + \$Shortages$$

$$= \$0 + \$2,000.00 + \$1,000.00$$

$$= \$3,000.00$$

Step 2 Find the planned purchases (see *equation 5.10*).

$$\$Pl.\ Purch. = \$Sales + \$Red. + EOM\ Stock - BOM\ Stock$$

$$= \$117,000.00 + \$3,000.00 + \$48,000.00 - \$44,000.00$$

$$= \$124,000.00$$

Step 3 Find open-to-buy at retail (see *equation 5.12*).

$$OTB = Pl.\ Purch. - Merch.\ Rec'd. - Merch.\ on\ Ord.$$

$$= \$124,000.00 - \$100,000.00 - \$20,000.00$$

$$= \$4,000.00$$

Problem What is the KOTS Company's OTB at cost if the initial markup percentage is 52%?

Solution

$$OTB \ at \ Cost = OTB \ at \ Retail \left(\frac{Complement \ of \ Initial \ MU\%}{100\%} \right)$$

$$= \$4,000.00 \left(\frac{100\% - 52\%}{100\%} \right)$$

$$= \$4,000.00 \, (.48)$$

$$= \$1,920.00$$

Open-to-Buy for the Balance of the Period Using Book Inventory

As you proceed through a period, purchases are made and sales occur. Business may advance according to the plan laid out or there may be a sharp increase or decrease in sales. For a variety of reasons, a buyer must be able to assess the current position of the store or department and take appropriate action if necessary. A buyer should not wait until the end of a period to see what the new open-to-buy figure will be, but should adjust the plan to reflect these unanticipated changes. The most accurate way to calculate open-to-buy would be to take a physical inventory. However, this usually is not feasible during the season and most buyers rely on a running book inventory.

The only complication in finding open-to-buy is the calculation of the planned purchases for the balance of the period. This quantity must reflect: 1) the difference between the planned sales and the sales to date; 2) the difference between the planned reductions and the reductions already taken; and 3) the current stock level as recorded in the book inventory as opposed to the BOM stock. Because the current stock figure accounts for all merchandise received to date, there is no additional merchandise received to be accounted for in the open-to-buy equation.

The planned purchases for the balance of the period can be written as the difference between planned and actual sales plus the difference between the planned and actual reductions plus the EOM stock minus the current stock level as recorded in the book inventory. The open-to-buy becomes the updated planned purchase minus the merchandise on order, as shown in the following:

EQUATION 5.13

Bal. Pl. Purch. = Diff. $Sales + Diff. $Red. + EOM Stock − Current Stock

---

Problem

On June 17, Sandy Drummer discovers a fantastic deal on ladies' skirts. She wants to know what her OTB is so that she can take advantage of the offer. From her six-month merchandising plan, she finds that her planned sales for the month of June are $8,000, the BOM stock was $10,000, the EOM stock was $15,000, and the planned reductions were $700. She has recorded actual sales through June 16 of $5,000. The reductions actually taken total $200. The book inventory gives a retail stock of $14,000. What is her OTB at cost on June 16 if she has $1000 worth of merchandise on order and a 45% initial markup?

Solution   *Step 1* Find the mid-month balance for planned purchases.

$$Bal.\ Pl.\ Purch. = Diff.\ \$Sales + Diff.\ \$Red.$$
$$+ EOM\ Stock - Current\ Stock$$

$$= (\$8,000.00 - \$5,000.00)$$
$$+ (\$700.00 - \$200.00)$$
$$+ \$15,000.00 - \$14,000.00$$

$$= \$3,000.00 + \$500.00 + \$1,000.00$$

$$= \$4,500.00$$

Step 2 Find the open-to-buy.

$$OTB = Bal.\ Pl.\ Purch. - Merch.\ Rec'd - Merch.\ On\ Order$$

$$= \$4,500.00 - \$0 - \$1,000.00$$

$$= \$3,500.00$$

Step 3 Find the OTB at cost using the initial markup percentage.

$$OTB\ at\ Cost = OTB\ at\ Retail \left(\frac{Comp.\ of\ Init.\ MU\%}{100\%} \right)$$

$$= \$3,500.00 \left(\frac{100\% - 45\%}{100\%} \right)$$

$$= \$3,500.00\,(.55)$$

$$= \$1,925.00$$

Open-to-Buy for the Balance of the Period Calculating Current Stock

If the book inventory for a certain date is not available, the open-to-buy for the balance of the period can still be determined. The current stock level is calculated by adding the BOM stock figure to the merchandise received and subtracting the actual dollar sales and reductions, as demonstrated in the following formula:

EQUATION 5.14

$$Current\ Stock = BOM\ Stock + Merch.\ Rec'd - Act.\ \$Sales - Act.\ \$Red.$$

Problem   The music department is selling more merchandise than anticipated due to a new young teen idol. The buyer would like to place some quick fill-in orders but the book inventory is not available. The planned sales for the month are $14,000, while actual sales to date are $7,500. The planned reductions were $900, while the actual reductions are $600. The buyer began the month with $8,000 in stock and planned to end the month with a $6,000 stock level. The department has received $9,000 in merchandise and $1,000 more is on order. What is the open-to-buy at retail for the balance of the month?

Solution   Method I

Step 1 Find the current stock level.

$$Current\ Stock = BOM\ Stock + Merch.\ Rec'd - Act.\ \$Sales - Act.\ Red.$$

$$= \$8,000.00 + \$9,000.00 - \$7,500.00 - \$600.00$$

$$= \$8,900.00$$

Step 2 Find the planned purchases for the balance of the month.

$$Bal.\ Pl.\ Purch. = \$Sales\ Diff. + \$Red.\ Diff. + EOM\ Stock - Current\ Stock$$

$$= (\$14,000.00 - \$7,500.00) + (\$900.00 - \$600.00)$$
$$+ (\$6,000.00 - \$8,900.00)$$

$$= \$6,500.00 + \$300.00 + \$6,000.00 - \$8,900.00$$

$$= \$3,900.00$$

Step 3 Find the open-to-buy at retail.

$$OTB = Bal.\ Pl.\ Purch. - Merch.\ Rec'd - Merch.\ on\ Order$$

$$= \$3,900.00 - \$0 - \$1,000.00$$

$$= \$2,900.00$$

In the next example, notice that the equation for BOM open-to-buy (see *equation 5.12*) gives the same solution.

Solution   Method II

Step 1 Find the planned purchases.

$$Pl.\ Purch. = Pl.\ Sales + Pl.\ Red. + EOM\ Stock - BOM\ Stock$$

$$= \$14,000.00 + \$900.00 + \$6,000.00 - \$8,000.00$$

$$= \$12,900.00$$

Step 2 Find the open-to-buy.

$$BOM\ OTB = Pl.\ Purch. - Merch.\ Rec'd - Merch.\ on\ Order$$

$$= \$12,900.00 - \$9,000.00 - \$1,000.00$$

$$= \$2,900.00$$

The result is the same because the actual dollar sales and reductions are subtracted and added in the same equation. These terms cancel each other out. Furthermore, the merchandise received is accounted for in the planned purchases.

Unit Open-to-Buy

Open-to-buy can be calculated in terms of units of merchandise instead of dollars. The formula is exactly the same as before:

$$Unit\ OTB = Unit\ Planned\ Purchases - Units\ Received - Units\ on\ Order$$

Many buyers find it convenient to talk in terms of the number of units of each item needed to fill fixtures or to meet the average unit sales in a classification. Generally, it is simply a matter of performing the calculations on an item basis rather than on dollar totals. The unit open-to-buy is helpful also when preparing a plan for staple merchandise using the week's supply method. Staple merchandise should always be on hand. The smallest quantity needed to satisfy customer demand is referred to commonly as the basic stock. This quantity often is cushioned by adding one week's extra stock, which becomes the reserve or safety factor. The open-to-buy is then the number of units on reserve plus the number of items usually sold during the delivery period plus the number of items sold during the reorder period minus the stock-on-hand minus the stock-on-order. The delivery period is the length of time between placing an order and the receipt of goods. The reorder period is the length of time between placement of orders. The formula for finding OTB number of units is:

EQUATION 5.15

$$OTB = Reserve + Delivery\ Per.\ Sales + Reorder\ Sales - Stock\text{-}on\text{-}Hand - Stock\text{-}on\text{-}Order$$

Problem In Townsend's, the sale of men's plain white T-shirts averages 30 per week. The store maintains a reserve of 60. Reorders are placed every four weeks and it takes about $1\frac{1}{2}$ weeks for a shipment to arrive. If the current stock is 93, and 36 are on order, what is the open-to-buy for the T-shirts?

Solution *Step 1* Calculate the number of sales per period.

$$Delivery\ Period\ Sales = \#Weeks\ for\ Delivery\ (Sales\ per\ Week)$$

$$= 1.5\,(30)$$

$$= 45$$

$$Reorder\ Period\ Sales = \#Weeks\ of\ Reorder\ (Sales\ per\ Week)$$

$$= 4\,(30)$$

$$= 120$$

Step 2 Calculate open-to-buy in units.

$$OTB = Reserve$$
$$+ Delivery\ Period\ Sales$$
$$+ Reorder\ Period\ Sales$$
$$- Stock\text{-}on\text{-}Hand$$
$$- Stock\text{-}on\text{-}Order$$
$$= 60 + 45 + 120 - 93 - 36$$
$$= 96$$

Computer Drill 24: Planning Open-to-Buy

Open-to-Buy is the name of the computer program that generates five types of problems for this section of the text. The types of problems available are:

- *BOM Open-to-Buy*
- *Open-to-Buy for the Balance of the Period*
- *Open-to-Buy for the Balance of the Period Using Book Inventory*
- *Open-to-Buy for the Balance of the Period Calculating Current Stock*
- *Unit Open-to-Buy*

Assignments

1. Laura Dalfun's merchandising plan for November has a planned beginning inventory of $41,000.00, and a closing inventory of $52,000.00. During this period, sales are estimated to be around $115,000.00, markdowns $2,200.00, and shortages $800.00. The store has received $60,000.00 in merchandise and $3,000.00 worth of stock is still on order. What is the open-to-buy at retail?

2. At First Avenue, the sale of blue jeans averages 27 pair a week. The store maintains a reserve of 62. Reorders are placed every 5 weeks and it takes 2 weeks for a shipment to arrive. If the current stock is 93 and 35 are on order, what is the open-to-buy for the blue jeans?

3. During July, First Avenue plans sales of $112,000.00 with markdowns of $2,200.00 and discounts of $1,100.00. The merchandising plan calls for a beginning inventory of $41,000.00 and a closing inventory of $50,000.00. What is First Avenue's open-to-buy at cost, if the initial markup percentage is 50.00%?

4. Laura Dalfun's buyer has retail stock of $11,700.00 for September and planned stock for the end of the month is $18,900.00. The buyer has received $1,200.00 in stock and has $1,200.00 on order. To date, the actual sales are $3,400.00 with markdowns totaling $3,000.00. If the planned sales for September were $8,200.00 and the planned reductions were $800.00, what is the open-to-buy for the balance of the month?

CHAPTER SIX

Maximizing Profit

The purpose of this book is to introduce mathematical tools that will aid in merchandise selection and selling by using quantitative and qualitative criteria. The final goal is to maximize profit via improved selection and selling. Sophisticated application of mathematical and projective techniques has not been explored fully in the area of retailing. This level of application can come only after the basics are mastered. You, as a potential buyer, must be willing to accept the challenge of a higher level of learning. To see how the concepts that you have learned can be utilized for maximizing profit, we will now examine the profit and loss statement in conjunction with the six-month merchandising plan.

There are various forms for profit and loss statements. Even though there is no standardized form, a buyer needs to be able to read the statement so the business can be analyzed and comparisons can be made. The profit and loss statement may be prepared annually, semi-annually, or monthly. For tax purposes, profit and loss statements must be prepared by the retailer or the retailer's accountant at least once a year. The statement provides a snapshot of business performance and offers a synopsis of key financial figures.

PROFIT AND LOSS STATEMENT

The **profit and loss statement** is a financial tool used to determine if a business has a profit or a loss. It also may be called the income statement or the operating statement, but no matter what it is called, it serves as a summary of business activities for a particular period. It projects, in capsule form, the interplay of sales, the cost of goods sold, and expenses, all of which determine the degree of profit or loss. When a loss is recorded, the bottom-line number may have a minus sign preceding it or it may be placed in parentheses or such brackets as these: <##>.

Simple Format of Profit and Loss Statements

The three basic components of the profit and loss statement are part of the six-month merchandising plan, that is, net sales, cost of goods sold, and expenses. Net sales and the cost of goods sold can be adjusted each month to improve the possibilities for attaining goals.

To determine the net profit or loss before taxes the gross margin must be calculated. Net sales minus the cost of goods sold equals gross margin. Then the expenses are subtracted from the gross margin to obtain net profit or loss. If expenses are greater than the gross margin, a negative number will result, which represents a loss. This concept is stated simply in the following statement:

EQUATION 6.1

$$\begin{array}{r} \textit{Net Sales} \\ - \ \underline{\textit{Cost of Goods Sold}} \\ \textit{Gross Margin} \\ - \ \underline{\textit{Expenses}} \\ \textit{Net Profit/Loss Before Taxes} \end{array}$$

Problem In comparing the profit and loss statements of two consecutive years for the McKnight Company, the owner noticed that the following changes had occurred:

Net Sales 1st year	$532,000
Net Sales up 11% in 2nd year	
Cost of Goods Sold maintained at	$295,000
Expenses 1st year	$250,000
Expenses up by 1% in 2nd year	

How has the net profit before taxes changed?

Solution *Step 1* Find the net profit or loss for the first year.

	1st Year
Net Sales	$532,000.00
− *Cost of Goods Sold*	−$295,000.00
Gross Margin	$237,000.00
− *Expenses*	−$250,000.00
Net Profit or Loss Before Taxes	− $13,000.00

Step 2 Find net sales by rewriting *equation 5.5*.

$$\textit{Variation\%} = \left(\frac{\textit{This Year} - \textit{Last Year}}{\textit{Last Year}} \right) 100\%$$

$$\textit{New} = (100\% + \textit{Variation\%}) \ \textit{Last Year}$$

$$= (100\% + 11\%) \ \$532,000.00$$

$$= (1.11) \ \$532,000.00$$

$$= \$590,520.00$$

Step 3 Find expenses from *equation 5.5.*

$$New = (100\% + Variation\%)\ Last\ Year$$

$$= (100\% + 1\%)\ \$250,000.00$$

$$= (1.01)\ \$250,000.00$$

$$= \$252,500.00$$

Step 4 Find the net profit or loss for the second year.

	2nd Year
Net Sales	$590,520.00
− *Cost of Goods Sold*	−$295,000.00
Gross Margin	$295,520.00
− *Expenses*	−$252,500.00
Net Profit or Loss Before Taxes	$43,020.00

The first year resulted in a deficit of $13,000. The second year resulted in profits of $43,020. This is an improvement of $56,020 in net profit before taxes over the one-year period.

Expanded Format

The format of the profit and loss statement is basic, however, variations can occur when the statement is expanded to include additional components. After the buyer becomes familiar with the format it is easy to see those records that must be kept and summarized to produce the statement.

The following profit and loss statement and the glossary of terms demonstrate, in greater detail, the interrelationship among the components used to derive operating profit or loss before taxes. From an accounting perspective, this information could be broken down into even smaller units of analysis. While the glossary of terms on the following page defines each component, the format for the profit and loss statement shown in Figure 6.1 illustrates additions and reductions to sales, cost of goods sold, and expenses to determine profit or loss.

FIGURE 6.2

Profit and Loss Statement

Gross Sales:		800,000	
Less: Sales, Returns, and Allowances	−65,000		
Sales Discounts	−15,000		
Net Sales –		720,000	
Cost of Goods Sold:			
Inventory (incl. transfers in/out), Feb. 1, 20_		95,000	
Gross Purchases	452,000		
Less: Ret. and Allow.	−12,000		
Net Purchases		+440,000	
Goods Available for Sale		535,000	
Inventory (incl. transfers in/out), Jan. 31, 20_		−110,000	
Cost of Goods Sold			−425,000
Gross Margin:			295,000
Operating Expenses:			
Fixed Expenses		120,000	
Variable Expenses		+ 80,000	
Total Operating Expenses			−200,000
Operating Profit or Loss Before Taxes			95,000

Glossary of Terms Included on a Profit and Loss Statement

Gross Sales All sales for the period obtained from record of sales.

Customer Returns and Allowances Merchandise that is returned to the retailer for full or partial credit.

Sales Discounts Discounts granted to employees and preferred customers.

Net Sales Gross sales minus returns and allowances minus discounts.

Inventory, Feb. 1, 20___ Physical inventory at the beginning of the period.

Gross Purchases All merchandise purchased by the company for resale during the period.

Returns to vendors Merchandise that is returned to the manufacturer or vendor for full or partial credit.

Net Purchases Gross purchases minus returns and allowances.

Inventory, Jan. 31, 20__ Physical inventory at the end of the period.

Cost of Goods Sold Beginning inventory plus net purchases minus ending inventory.

Gross Margin Net Sales minus cost of goods sold.

Fixed Expenses Expenses that are mandatory and reasonably consistent in the operation of the business.

Variable Expenses Expenses that are not essential to the business and could fluctuate or be manipulated to meet needs.

Total Operating Expenses Fixed expenses plus variable expenses.

Operating Profit or Loss Before Taxes Gross margin minus expenses (the net profit after taxes can be used for owner's revenue, reinvestment in business, dividends to stockholders, or repayment of debts.)

Please note: the profit and loss statement that follows will be used for all problems in this section.

Problem From the information provided in this sample, complete the profit and loss statement by calculating net sales, cost of goods sold, gross margin, total operating expenses, and profit or loss.

Gross Sales: $266,700

Customer Returns and Allowances	$22,000	
Customer Discounts	$ 5,000	
Net Sales		————

Cost of Goods Sold:

Inventory, Feb. 1, 20__		$32,000
Gross Purchases	$150,100	
Returns and Allowances	$ 4,000	
Net Purchases		$146,100
Goods Available for Sale		$178,100
Inventory, Jan. 31, 20__		$ 36,000
Cost of Goods Sold		————

Gross Margin   ————

Operating Expenses:

Fixed Expenses	$40,000	
Variable Expenses	$25,000	
Total Operating Expenses		————

Operating Profit or Loss Before Taxes   ————

Solution   *Step 1* Find the net sales figure.

$$\text{Net Sales} = \text{Gr. Sales} - \text{Cust. Ret. \& Allow.} - \text{Sales Disc.}$$

$$= \$266,700.00 - \$22,000.00 - \$5,000.00$$

$$= \$239,700.00$$

Step 2 Find the cost of goods sold.

$$\text{Cost of Goods Sold} = \text{End. Inv.} + (\text{Gr. Purch.} - \text{Cust. Ret. \& Allow.}) - \text{Beg. Inv.}$$

$$= \$32,000.00 + (\$150,100.00 - \$4,000.00) - \$36,000.00$$

$$= \$142,100.00$$

Step 3 Find the gross margin.

$$GM = Net\ Sales - Cost\ of\ Goods\ Sold$$

$$= \$239,700.00 - \$142,100.00$$

$$= \$97,600.00$$

Step 4 Find the total operating expenses.

$$Oper.\ Exp. = Fixed\ Exp. + Var.\ Exp.$$

$$= \$40,000.00 + \$25,000.00$$

$$= \$65,000.00$$

Step 5 Find operating profit or loss before taxes.

$$Oper.\ Profit\ or\ Loss = GM - Total\ Oper.\ Exp.$$

$$= \$97,600.00 - \$65,000.00$$

$$= \$32,600.00$$

Methods of Maximizing Profit

To augment the operating profit, often it is not enough to determine just the profit or loss. The buyer needs to analyze the profit and loss statement to determine ways to increase the operating profit. The format of the profit and loss statement shows that the three fundamental ways in which a buyer might increase the operating profit are: 1) increasing net sales; 2) decreasing cost of goods sold; and 3) reducing expenses. The discussion that follows will highlight the impact of each of these elements in the profit and loss statement and will assume that the other two elements do not change dramatically. However, all three types of changes can occur simultaneously.

In the first alternative, net sales are increased, while the cost of goods sold and operating expenses remain relatively stable. Sales can be increased by using additional advertising or promotion efforts. However, if this is done, the expense portion of the statement probably will increase unless other expenses are reduced. The increased sales results from this advertising or promotion must outweigh the additional expenses involved.

The six-month merchandising plan is a valuable resource in evaluating sales trends. A decline in dollar sales volume or in the number of sales transactions can be detected immediately from sales figures (from sales reports) and the merchandising plan can be adjusted. The markup and markdown portions of the six-month merchandising plan also may be examined to determine if the markup percentage should be increased or if markdowns may be greater than anticipated.

Sales also can be increased by reviewing the needs and wants of the customer. A buyer can supply new merchandise lines, revamp some existing lines, and eliminate others, all of which can help. In the process of investing in new or different merchandise, a buyer should remember that the cost of the merchandise has to remain stable or decrease to be able to increase the profit margin. If the process of examination of sales is continuous and appropriate action is taken when a problem is identified, the chances of increasing the profit are much greater than when left to chance.

In the second alternative for improving the profit margin, the cost of goods sold is decreased substantially while sales and operating expenses are improved or remain stable. The most obvious method of accomplishing this would be to spend less on the merchandise purchased. This might be possible by receiving quantity discounts and taking advantage of cash discounts more frequently, or by seeking out manufacturers with comparable quality goods offered at a lower price. However, a buyer should be aware that by attempting to decrease the cost of goods there may be a decrease in sales because of a decline in quality. Again, the six-month merchandising plan is helpful for keeping track of the cost of merchandise. The plan can serve as a method for controlling costs and improving the financial picture.

The third alternative for increasing net profits is to reduce expenses. Some expenses are fixed or not flexible, such as rent. Rent must be paid and it is an expense over which you (as a retailer) have limited control. It is paid once a month, and is a consistent amount. Conversely, office supplies are a variable expense for which you can have significant control. There is no set amount that must be spent each month. If you want to reduce expenses there may be some office supplies that can be cut from the office supplies purchases. Additionally, a portion of the labor expense can be placed under fixed expenses, which implies minimum sales staffing. The balance of labor can be identified as a variable expense.

These three alternatives discussed are quite basic. There are many other factors that also can play a part in increasing profits. Each factor cannot occur in a void from the others because all the factors are interrelated. It is evident that all portions of the profit and loss statement will change from period to period. The entire statement, as well as its components, must be examined to determine whether or not profits will be increased. The retailers' goal is to maximize profits and the methods of attaining this goal are numerous.

To assess the impact of the improvement on the profit margin, we will compare a new statement with an old statement. For the next three problems, you will use the same profit and loss information as presented on page 195. One problem will demonstrate what happens when all figures remain constant and sales are changed, another will demonstrate what happens when only cost of goods sold changes in value, and the last one will show the impact when only the expense figure is altered. To find the dollar amount of the impact, take the difference between this year's profit/loss figure and last year's profit/loss figure, as shown in the following:

EQUATION 6.3

$$\$Impact = \$This\ Year's\ Profit/Loss\ Figure - \$Last\ Year's\ Profit/Loss\ Figure$$

Problem   Given the information supplied on page 195, what impact would a reduction in gross sales to $233,700.00 have on the operating profit?

Solution   *Step 1* Find the net sales figure.

$$Net\ Sales = Gr.\ Sales - Cust.\ Ret.\ \&\ Allow. - Sales\ Disc.$$

$$= \$233,700.00 - \$22,000.00 - \$5,000.00$$

$$= \$206,700.00$$

Step 2 Find the operating profit or loss.

$$Operating\ Profit/Loss = Net\ Sales - Cost\ of\ Goods\ Sold - Expenses$$

$$= \$206{,}700.00 - \$142{,}100.00 - \$65{,}000.00$$

$$= -\$400.00\ (This\ is\ a\ loss\ figure.)$$

Step 3 To find the dollar impact, compare this new operating loss with the previous operating profit or loss.

$$\$Impact = This\ Year's - Last\ Year's$$

$$= -\$400.00 - \$32{,}600.00$$

$$= -\$33{,}000.00$$

The business moved from $32,600 profit to a $400 loss. This is a decline of $33,000.

Problem Again, using the information given on page 195, what impact would an increase to $153,000 in the cost of goods sold have on the operating profit?

Solution **Step 1** Find the operating profit.

$$Oper.\ Profit = Net\ Sales - Cost\ of\ Goods\ Sold - Exp.$$

$$= \$239{,}700.00 - \$153{,}000.00 - \$65{,}000.00$$

$$= \$21{,}700.00$$

Step 2 To find the impact, compare the change in operating profit (see equation 6.3).

$$\$Impact = New - Old$$

$$= \$21{,}700.00 - \$32{,}600.00$$

$$= -\$10{,}900.00$$

The $32,600 operating profit has been reduced to $21,700. This represents a decline of $10,900.

Problem Given the information supplied on page 195, what impact would a reduction in expenses to $55,000 have on operating profit?

Solution **Step 1** Find the operating profit.

$$Operating\ Profit = Net\ Sales - Cost\ of\ Goods\ Sold - Expenses$$

$$= \$239{,}700.00 - \$142{,}100.00 - \$55{,}000.00$$

$$= \$42{,}600.00$$

Step 2 To find the dollar impact, compare the new operating profit with the previous figure.

$$\$Impact = This\ Year's - Last\ Year's$$

$$= \$42,600.00 - \$32,600.00$$

$$= \$10,000.00$$

The operating profit was $32,600 and is now $42,600, an increase of $10,000.

Computer Drill 25: Profit and Loss Statement

Profit and Loss Statement is the name of the computer program that generates three types of problems for this section of the text. The types of problems available are:

- *Simple Format of Profit and Loss Statements*
- *Expanded Format*
- *Methods of Maximizing Profit*

Assignments

1. A confidential report circulated to all department managers in the Lunplat Store provided net sales, gross margin, and operating profit figures for each department. One of the managers had anticipated a larger operating profit and felt that either the cost of goods sold or the operating expenses might have been calculated incorrectly. Reconstruct the profit and loss statement as the department manager might have done to check the figures. The net sales were given as $53,872.00, the gross margin as $45,812.00, and the operating profit as $21,732.00. Was the department manager right in thinking that the figures had been calculated incorrectly?

Profit and Loss Statement

Net Sales	_____
Cost of Goods Sold	_____
Gross Margin	_____
Total Operating Expenses	_____
Operating Profit or Loss Before Taxes	_____

2. Using this same profit and loss statement, what impact would a change to $32,772.00 in total operating expenses have on the operating profit?

3. A department in Hopewell's Store grossed $33,000.00 in sales with $264.00 in customer returns and $1,320.00 in customer discounts. The total cost of goods sold was $4,556.00, while the variable and fixed expenses totaled $13,860.00. Enter the data for each line in the form of the profit and loss statement.

Profit and Loss Statement

Net Sales	_____
Cost of Goods Sold	_____
Gross Margin	_____
Total Operating Expenses	_____
Operating Profit or Loss Before Taxes	_____

4. Last year, Pinedale's grossed sales of $114,000.00 with customer returns of $684.00 and discounts of $2,280.00. The gross purchases were $21,660.00 with returns to vendors of $649.00. The inventory began with $20,520.00 worth of merchandise and ended with $36,480.00 in inventory. The fixed expenses totaled $32,957.00, while the variable expenses were $22,903.00. Construct the profit and loss statement, using the blank statement below.

Profit and Loss Statement

Gross Sales: ————

Less:

Sales, Returns, and Allowances ————

Sales Discounts ————

   Net Sales ————

Cost of Goods Sold:

*Inventory, Feb. 1, 20_* ————

Gross Purchases ————

Less: Returns and Allowances. ————

Net Purchases ————

Goods Available for Sale ————

*Inventory, Jan. 31, 20_* ————

   Cost of Goods Sold ————

   Gross Margin ————

Operating Expenses:

Fixed Expenses ————

Variable Expenses ————

Total Operating Expenses ————

Operating Profit or Loss Before Taxes ————

5. In many situations, a retailer may not compile a profit and loss statement for individual departments. For your own information, you decide to create a statement for your department. Gross sales are $35,000.00, sales discounts at $700.00, net sales are $33,985.00, beginning inventory is $2,100.00, ending inventory is $11,550.00, net purchases are $5,494.00, returns and allowances are $106.00, fixed expenses at $9,212.00, and total expenses are $19,600.00. Using this information, complete the profit and loss statement below.

Profit and Loss Statement

Gross Sales: _____

Less:

Sales, Returns, and Allowances _____

Sales Discounts _____

    Net Sales _____

Cost of Goods Sold:

*Inventory, Feb. 1, 20_* _____

Gross Purchases _____

Less: Returns and Allowances. _____

Net Purchases _____

Goods Available for Sale _____

*Inventory, Jan. 31, 20_* _____

    Cost of Goods Sold _____

    Gross Margin _____

Operating Expenses:

Fixed Expenses _____

Variable Expenses _____

Total Operating Expenses _____

Operating Profit or Loss Before Taxes _____

---

6. How much would the operating profit change if the gross sales were $42,703.00?

Reference Readings

Bohlinger, Maryanne Smith, *Merchandise Buying – Principles and Application*, Wm. C. Brown Company, 1990

Hartley, Robert F., *Retailing – Challenge and Opportunity*, Houghton Mifflin Company, Boston, 1984

Packard, Sidney, Arthur A. Winters, and Nathan Axelrod, *Fashion Buying and Merchandising*, Fairchild Publications, Inc., New York, 1983

Shipp, Ralph D., *Retail Merchandising Principles and Applications*, Houghton-Mifflin Company, Boston, 1985

Shuch, Milton L., *Retail Buying and Merchandising*, Prentice-Hall, Inc., New Jersey, 1988

Tepper, Bette K., and Newton E. Godnik, *Mathematics for Retail Buying, Fourth Edition*, Fairchild Publications, Inc., New York, 1994

Answers to Assignments

Chapter One

Pages 12–14
1. $115.00
2. $21.00
3. $65.71 (price at $65.95, $65.99, $66 depending on pricing policies)
4. 44%
5. 90%
6. $110.63
7. $13.49
8. $82.00
9. $101.00
10. $76.50
11. $48.00

Pages 18–19
1. $4,828.37
2. $1,024.51
3. $19,018.96

Pages 36–38
1. $2,016.00
2. 38.55%
3. $124.11
4. $11,142.86
5. 7.5
6. $3,528.57
7. $1,640.00
8. $4,920.00

Page 44
1. $2,265.00
2. 37%
3. $1,093.49
4. $1,251.29

Page 49
1. $19,007.60
2. 43%
3. 56.17%

Page 54
1. $210.57
2. 35.74%
3. 20.44%

Chapter Two

Page 59
1. 15%
2. $25.60
3. $55.00

Pages 73–76
1. $2.00
2. $18.00
3. $595.00
4. $166.00
5. 7%
6. 11%
7. 8.3%
8. 10.1%
9. $42.00
10. $577.50
11. $585.00
12. 17.65%
13. 17.65%
14. 7.53%

Chapter Three

Pages 81–82
1. $538.35
2. $0
3. $1,905.12
4. $2,228.52
5. $100.59

Page 85
1. $4,203.00
2. $2,521.54
3. $61.14
4. $115.71

Pages 88–89
1. June 10
2. May 10
3. $3,992.85
4. October 22
5. January 10

Page 92
1. $3,353.00
2. $20.38
3. $1,891.00
4. $77.14

Pages 96–97
1. $360.00
2. $15.30
3. $5,948.00
4. $273.00
5. $2,355.78

Page 102
1. $468.00
2. $714.89
3. $12.92

Page 108
1. $84.24
2. $51.47
3. $127.12
4. $73.00

Pages 110–113
1. $2,573.00
2. $333.90
3. $305.35
4. $4,255.00
5. March 27
6. $39.90
7. $21.00

8. 0.0
9. $4,203.00
10. $7.35
11. $11.90
12. $567.36
13. June 24
14. $262.50
15. $17.36

Chapter Four

Pages 121–122
1. $11,460.00
2. $331.00
3. 4.64%
4. $51,997.00
5. $2,080.00
6. 3.10%

Pages 132–133
1. 5.00
2. $1,300.00
3. $11,700.00
4. 3.00
5. 7.00
6. 6.00
7. 3.02
8. 8.00

Pages 136–137
1. 8.10
2. $22,600.00
3. $56,430.00
4. $5,140.00
5. 3.70
6. $11,100.00

Chapter Five

Pages 160–161
1. $35,120.40
2. $22,425.00
3. $24,840.00
4. $47,960.00
5. $46,104.00

Page 168
1. Basic Stock = $5,559.60;
   %Variation = $3,932.40
2. $1,860.00
3. $4,188.40
4. $20,184.00

Pages 175–177

1. 10.64%

2. $5,434.00

3. $6,292.00

4. $2,176.00

5. 34%

6. 35%

7. 25%

Pages 181–182

1. $199,800.00

2. $10,340.00

3. $186,500.00

4. $47,700.00

5. $56,000.00

Page 190

1. $66,000.00

2. 123

3. $62,150.00

4. $13,800.00

Chapter Six

Pages 200–202

1. $53,872.00; $8,060.00; $45,812.00; $24,080.00; $21,732.00

2. −$8,692.00

3. $31,416.00; $4,556.00; $26,860.00; $13,860.00; $13,000.00

4. $114,000.00; $684.00; $2,280.00; $111,036.00; $20,520.00; $21,660.00; $649.00; $21,011.00; $41,531.00; $36,480.00; $5,051.00; $105,985.00; $32,957.00; $22,903.00; $55,860.00; $50,125.00

5. $35,000.00; $315.00; $700.00; $33,985.00; $2,100.00; $5,600.00; $106.00; $5,494.00; $7,594.00; $11,550.00; −$3,956.00; $37,941.00; $9,212.00; $10,388.00; $19,600.00; $18,341.00

6. $7,703.00

Index